How I Reversed Time

Dennis Joseph

This book was designed specifically to be used with **coloring pencils** and/or **crayons**. While I personally love markers, to avoid bleeding, it would be in your best interest to place a sheet underneath the page before coloring anything. By the end of the book, you'll have the opportunity to draw/sketch/color in 3 of your OWN thoughts/ideas. Share them on social media. I'd love to see what you come up with!

Copyright © 2017 Dennis Joseph

All rights reserved.

ISBN: 1976121515
ISBN-13: 978-1976121517

WELCOME!

For the Adults:

For as long as I can remember, I've always wanted a super power. Super heroes and their ability to accomplish amazing feats always intrigued me. Unfortunately, I went through all of my teenage years and was never bitten by a radioactive spider, nor had the funds to build a super powered suit. It wasn't until I became an adult that I realized I didn't need either one (Although, they'd be great). I had a super power. The ability to reverse time. Not in a practical sense where I could physically revisit a random moment and change the course of history forever. No, more like I can revert your mood back to a happier time when life was as simple as just having to stay within the lines.

You ever wondered why adult coloring books are even called "adult" coloring books? It's partly because coloring, in general, is looked upon as something mainly kids do. We all have to grow up, but no one ever said your imagination has to age too. In my opinion, one of the keys to staying young is constantly feeding your creativity and keeping your imagination sprightly. As you make your way through many of my own random 140 character thoughts and submerge yourself within my world, I hope you discover some random ideas of your own. I hope you start listening to your own inner child more often. I hope you tap into your own abilities and remain as young, joyful and creative as your imagination will allow. I'll certainly be waiting to see that.

For the Kids:

Stay within the lines!

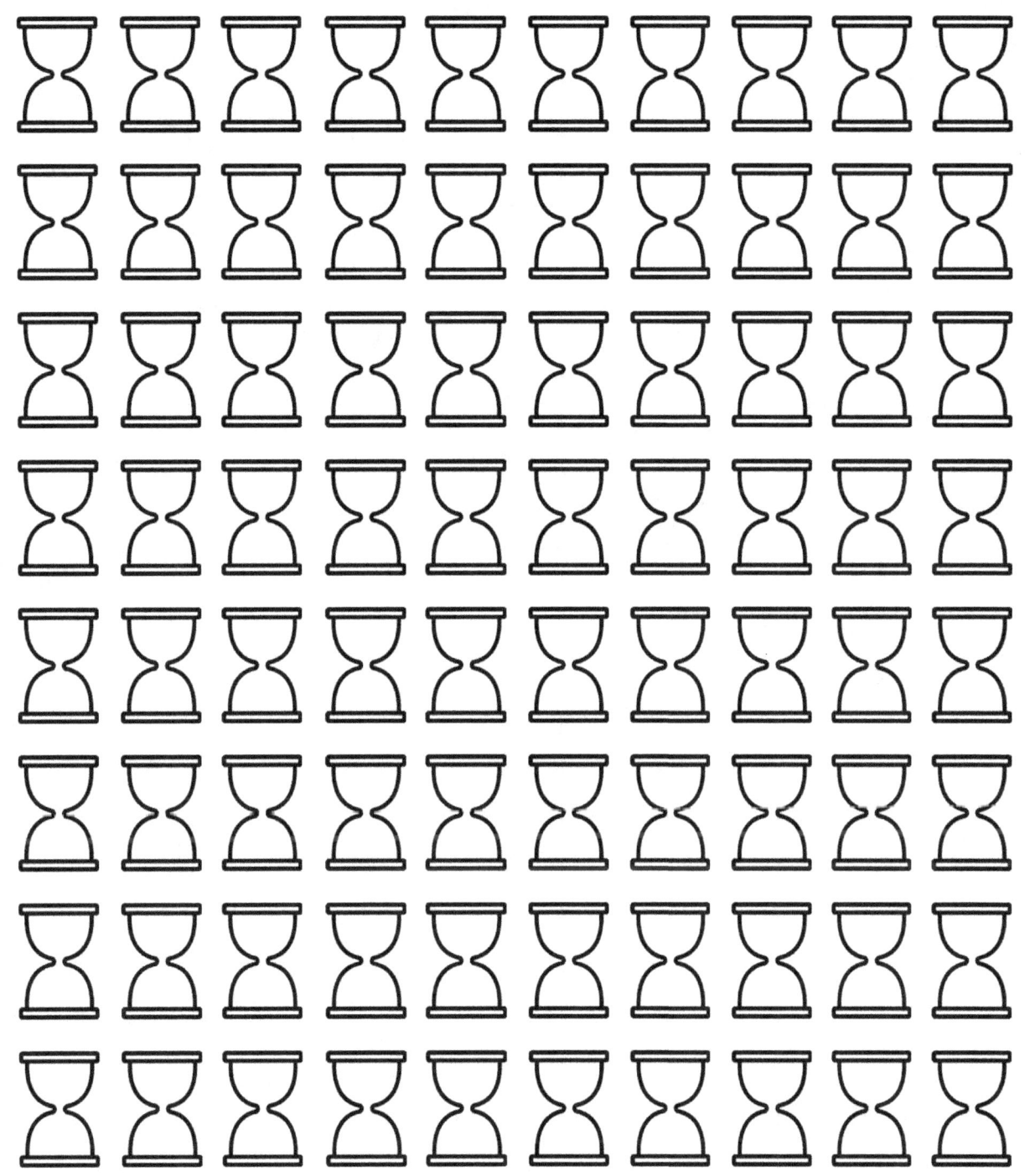

"TESTING..TESTING.."

Use these hourglasses to test out your Crayons, Coloring Pencils and/or Markers!

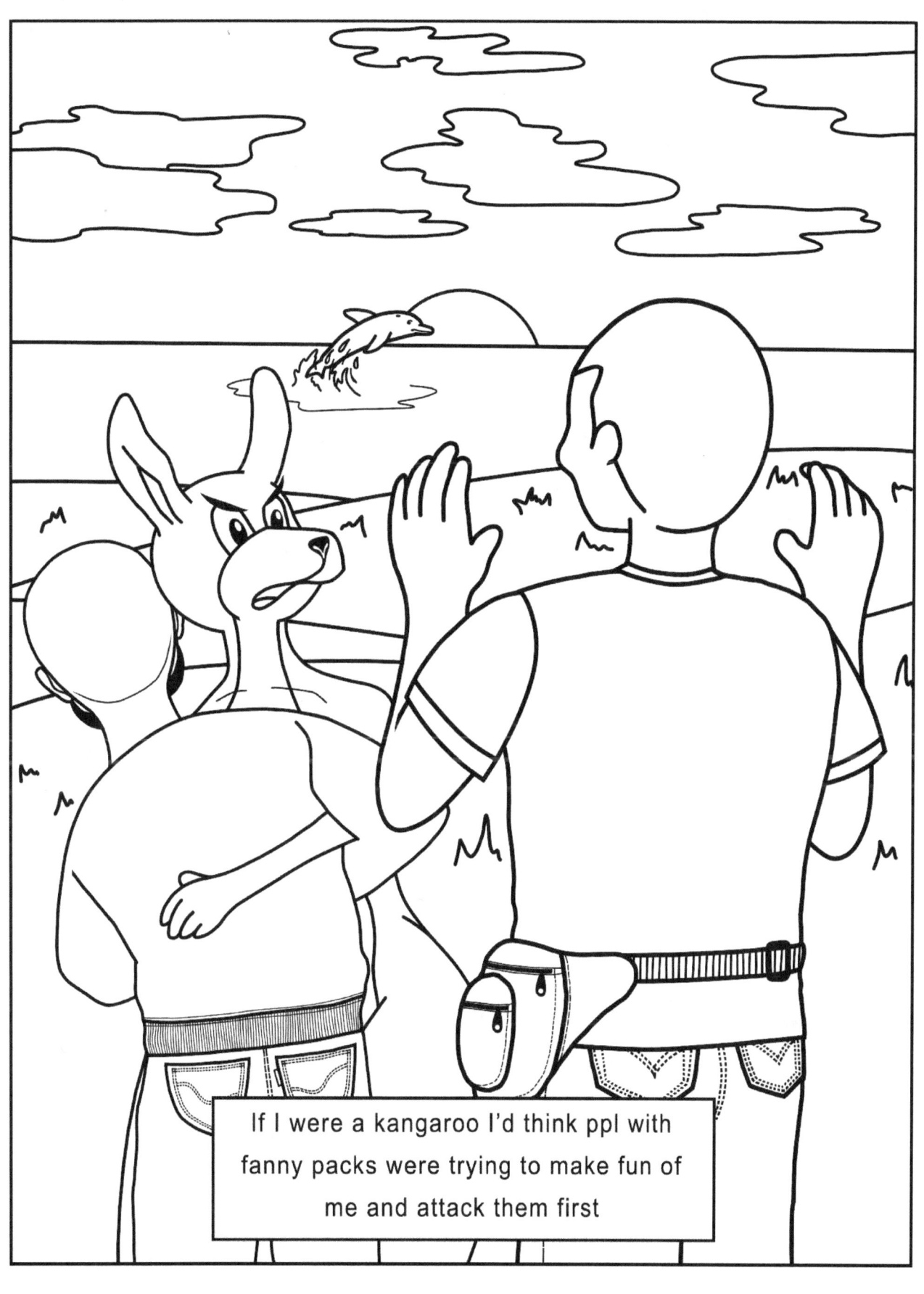

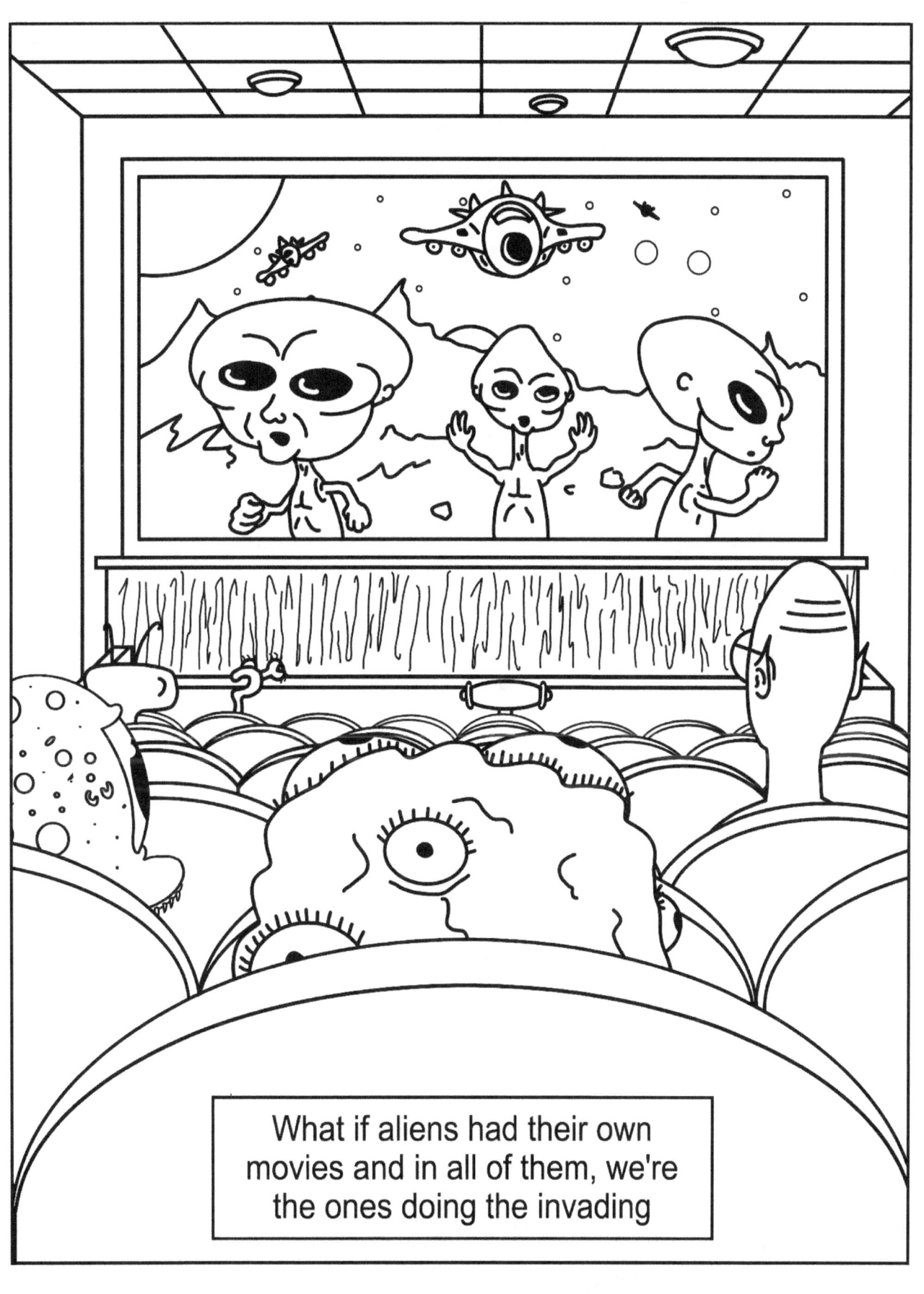

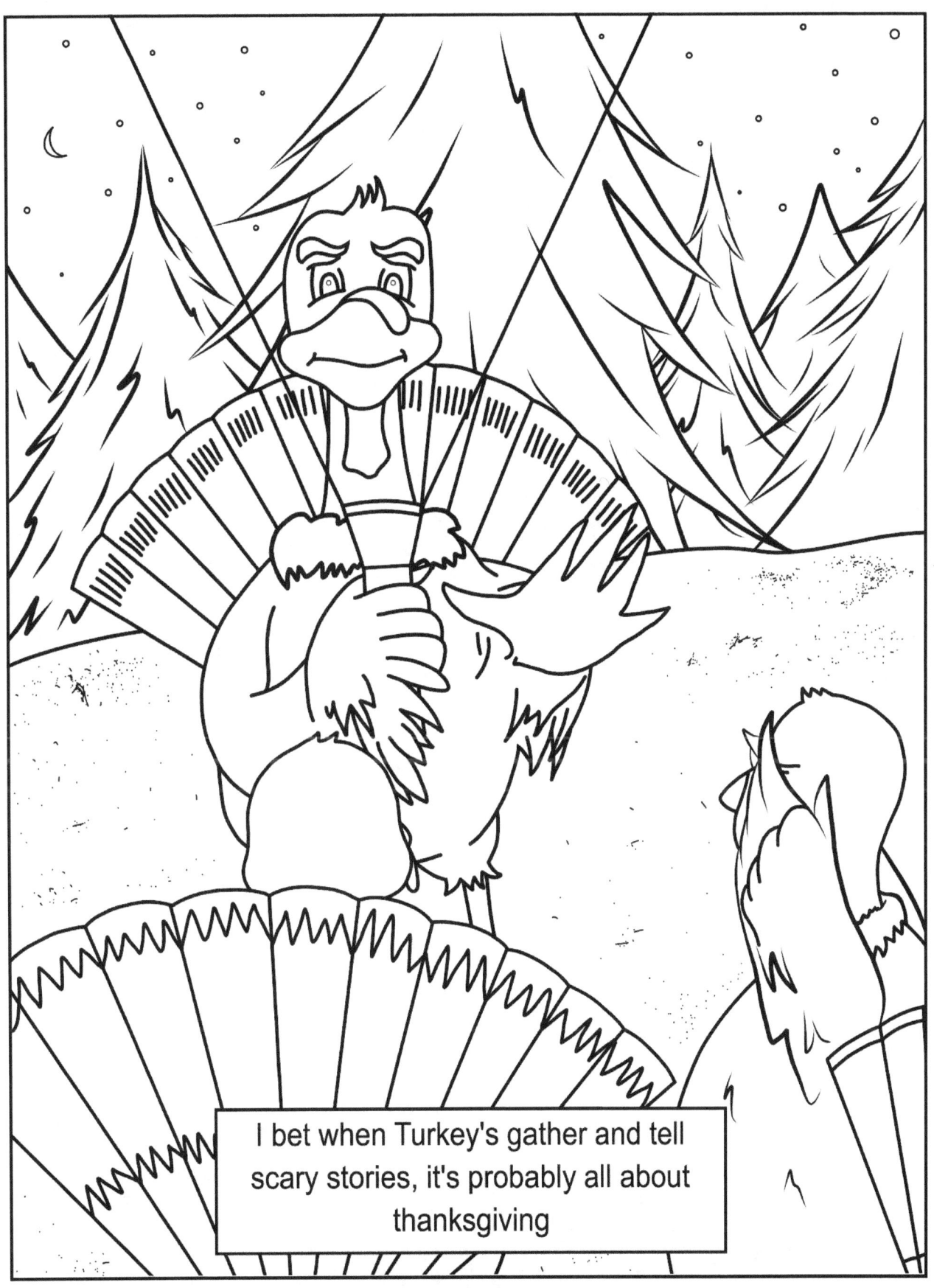

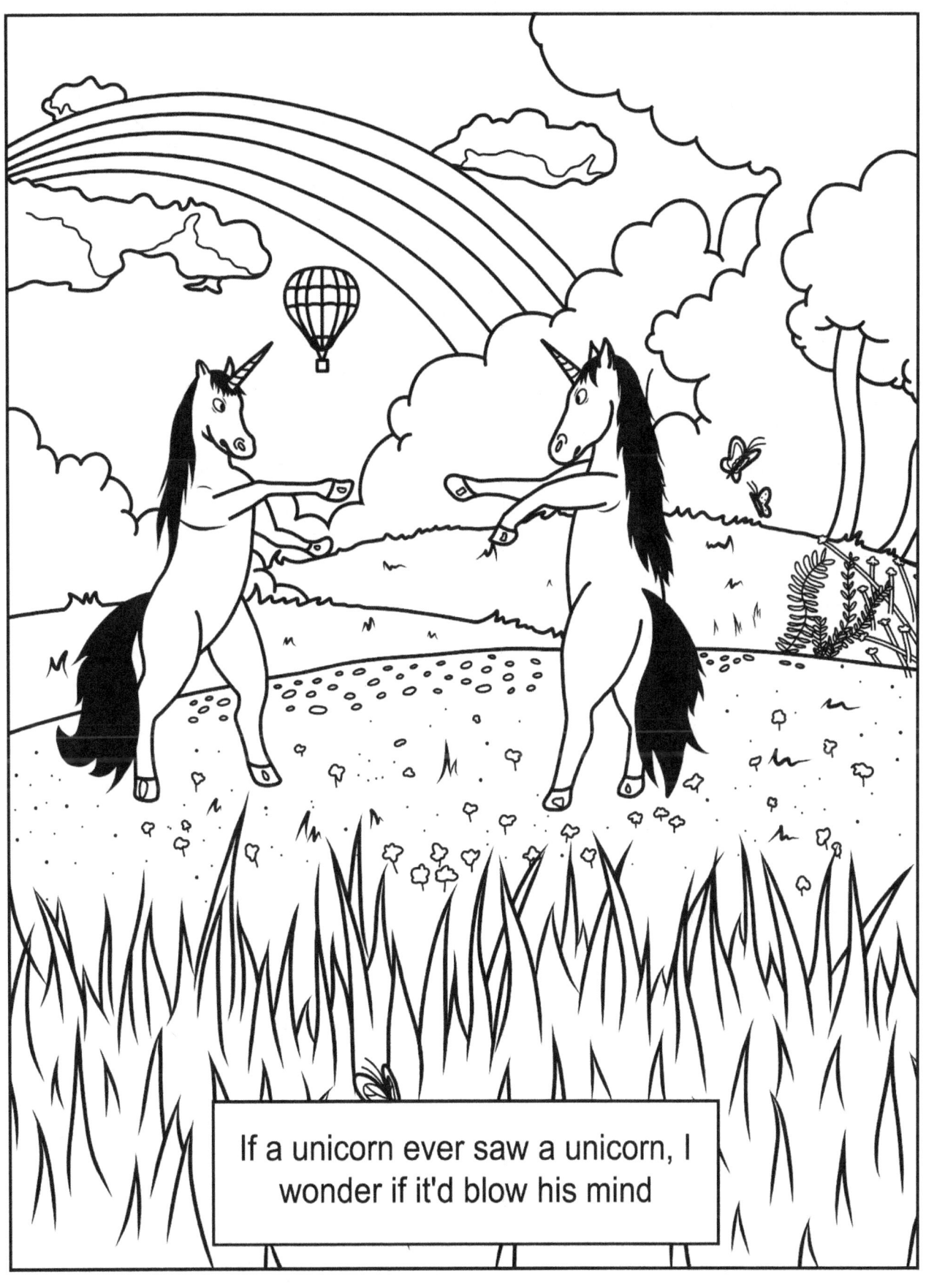

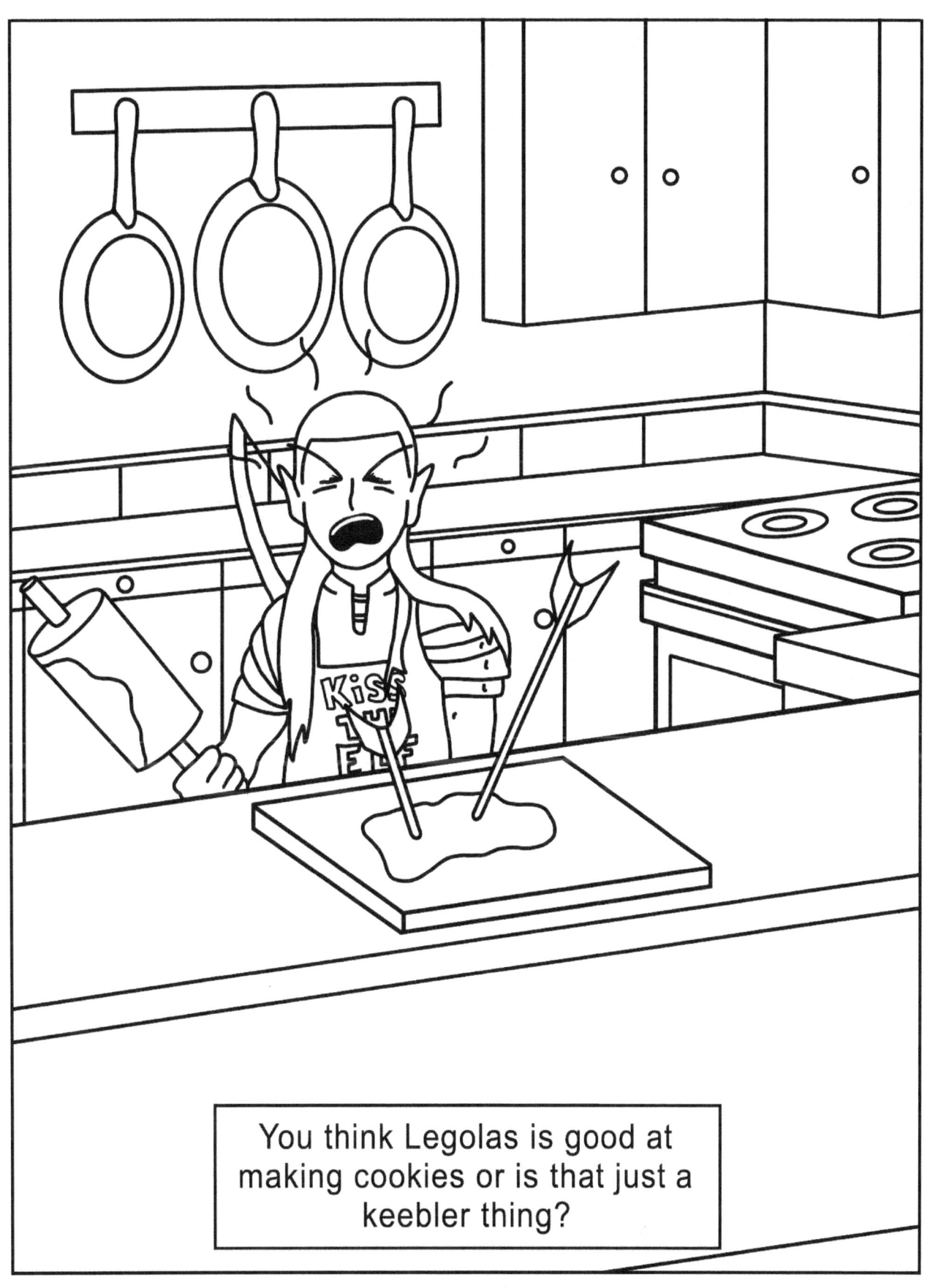

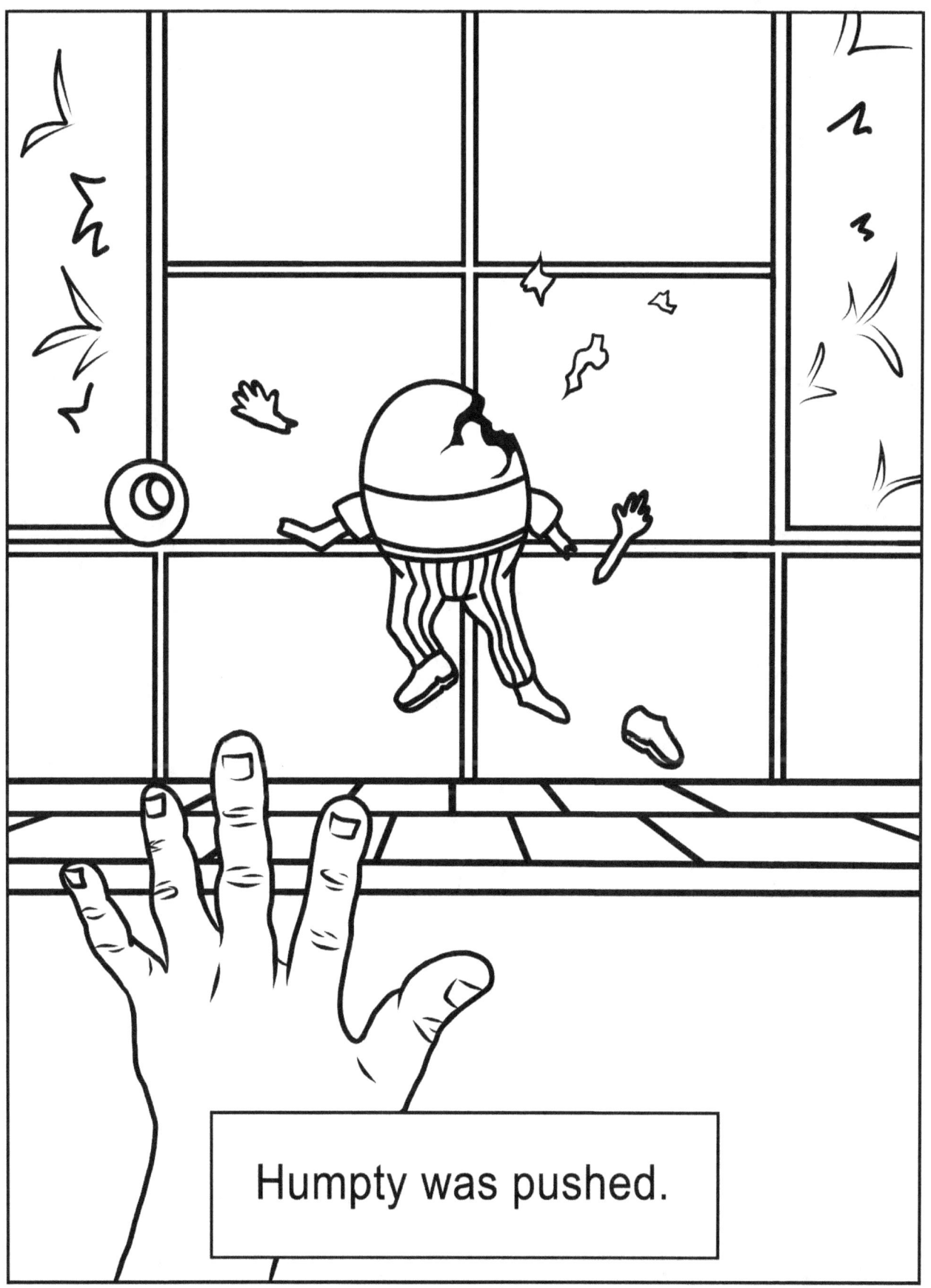

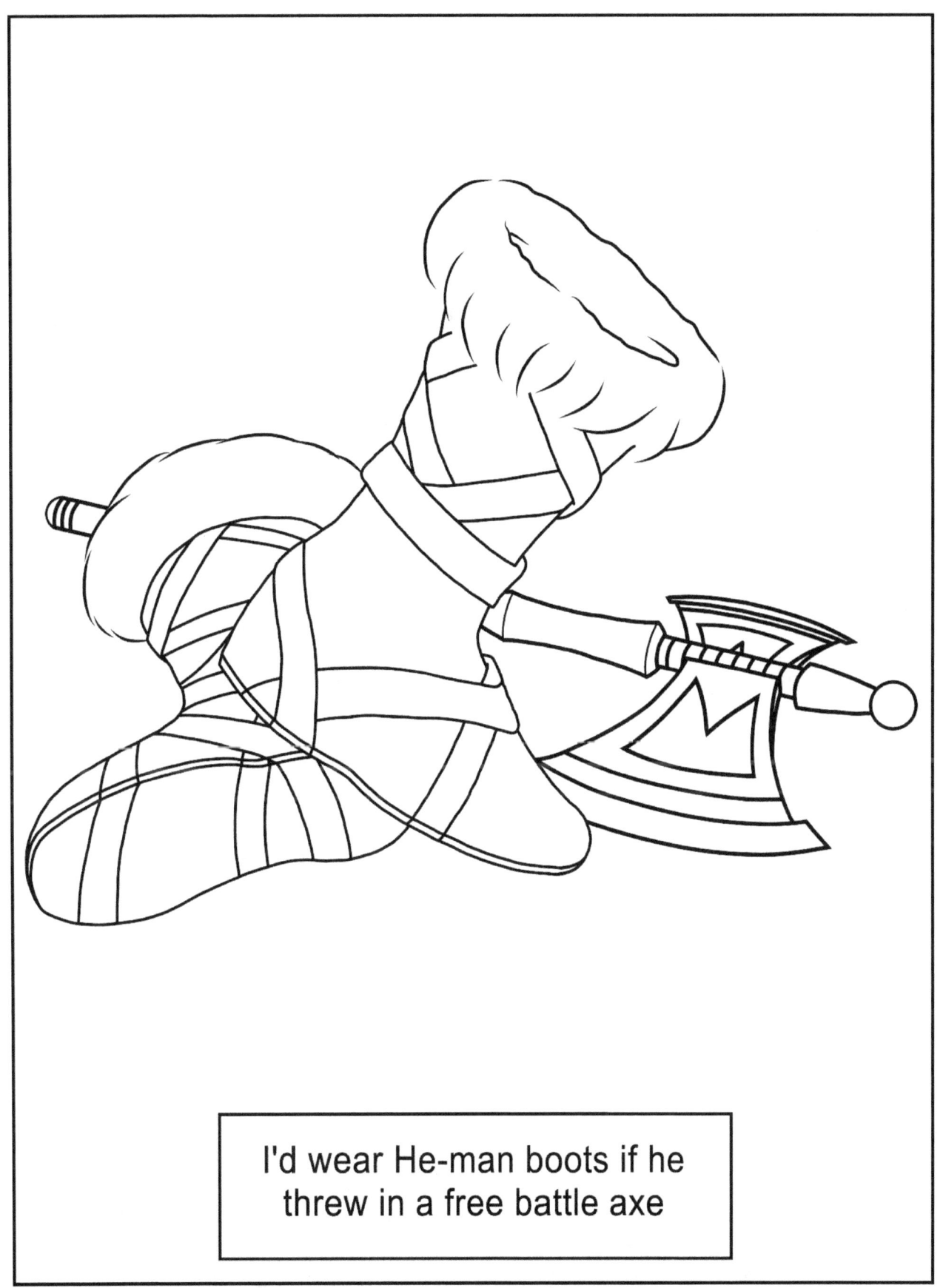

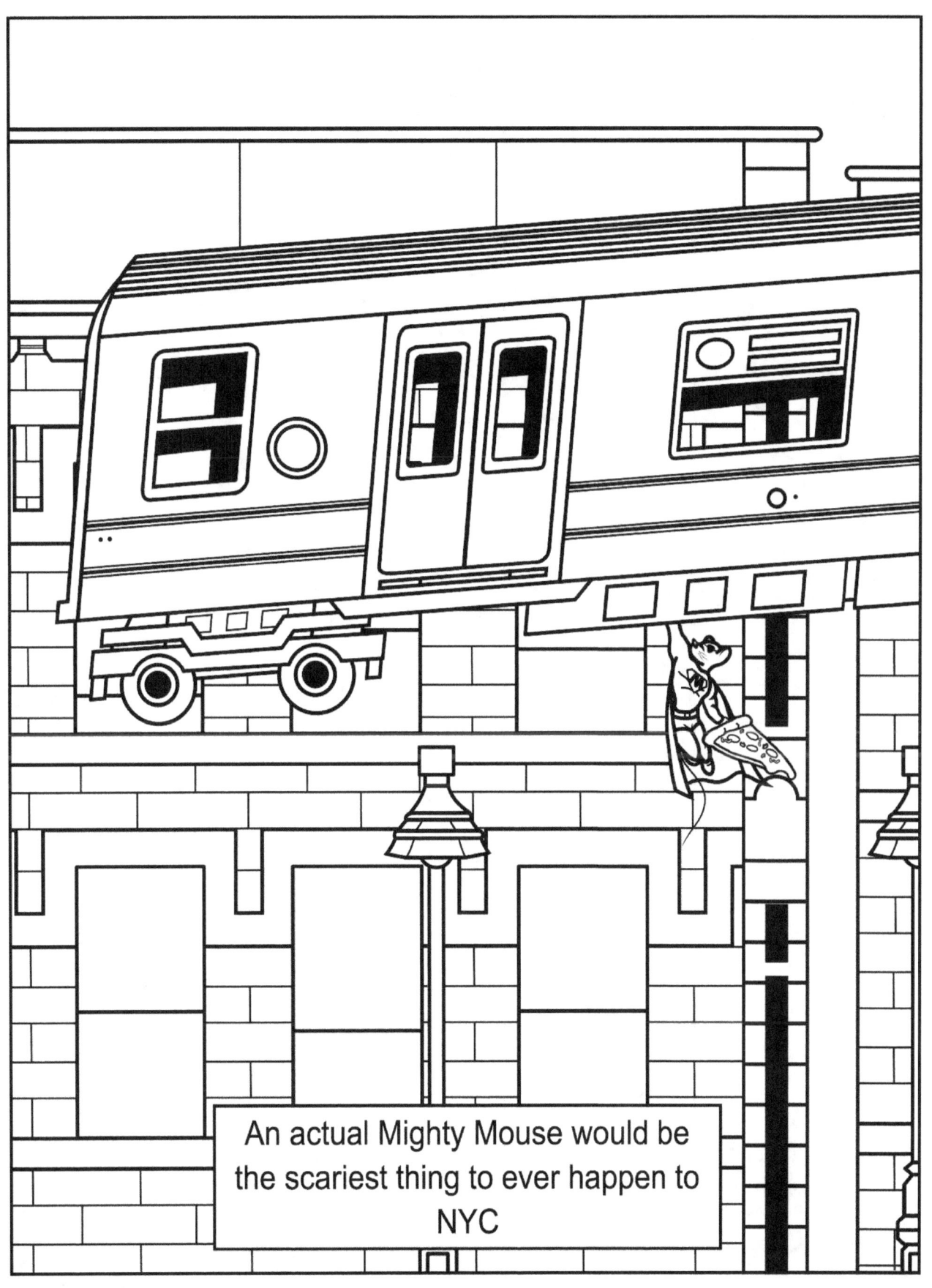

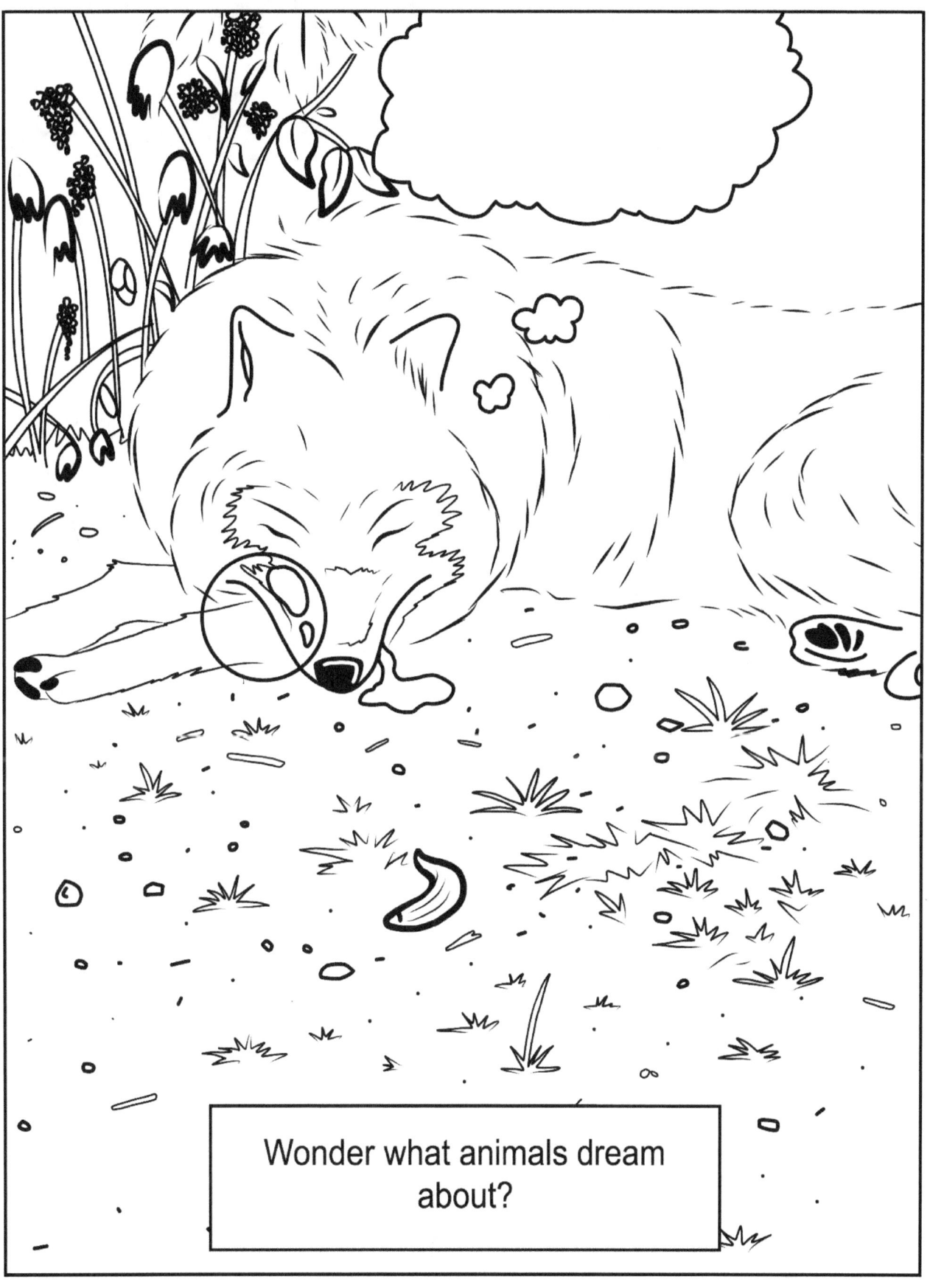

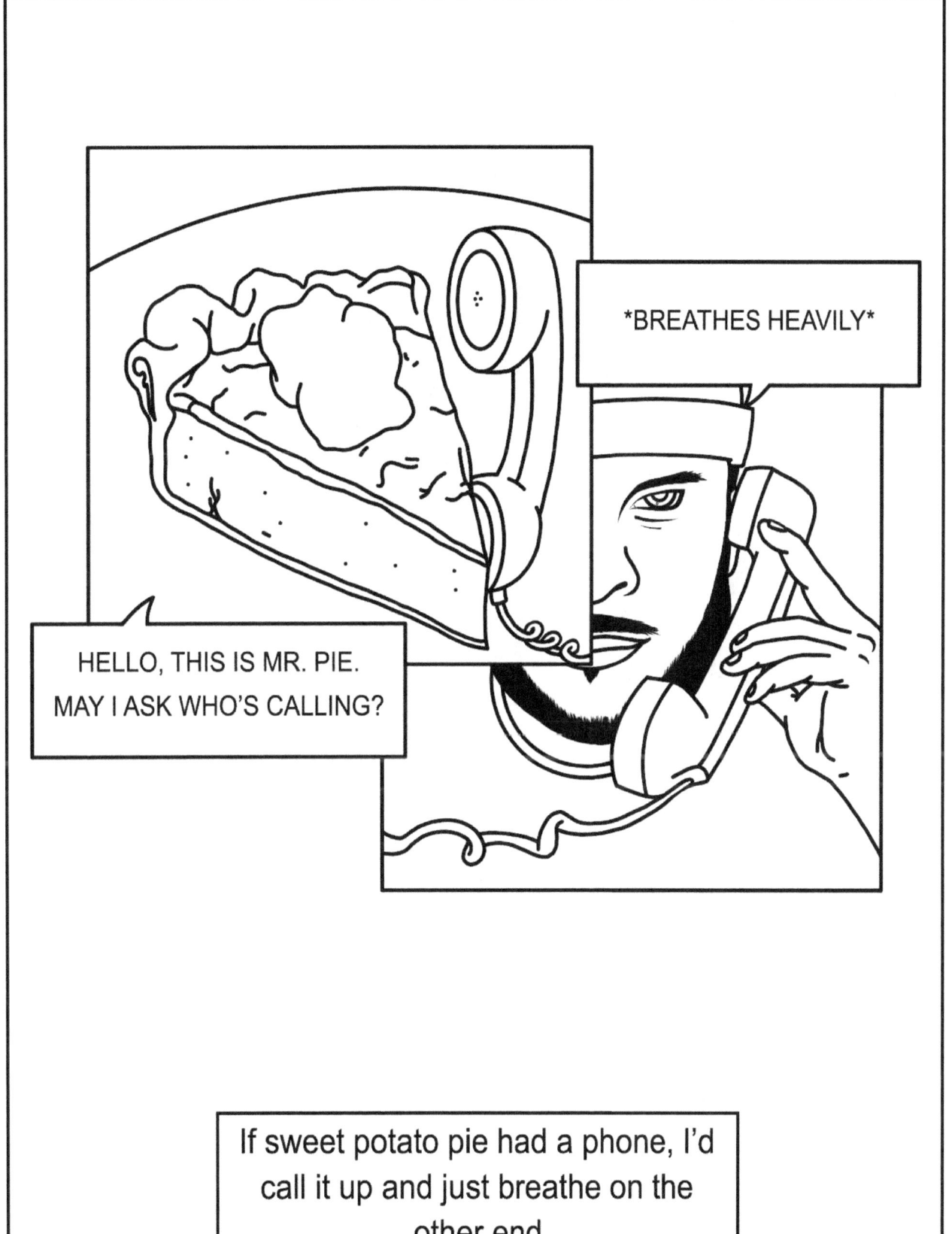

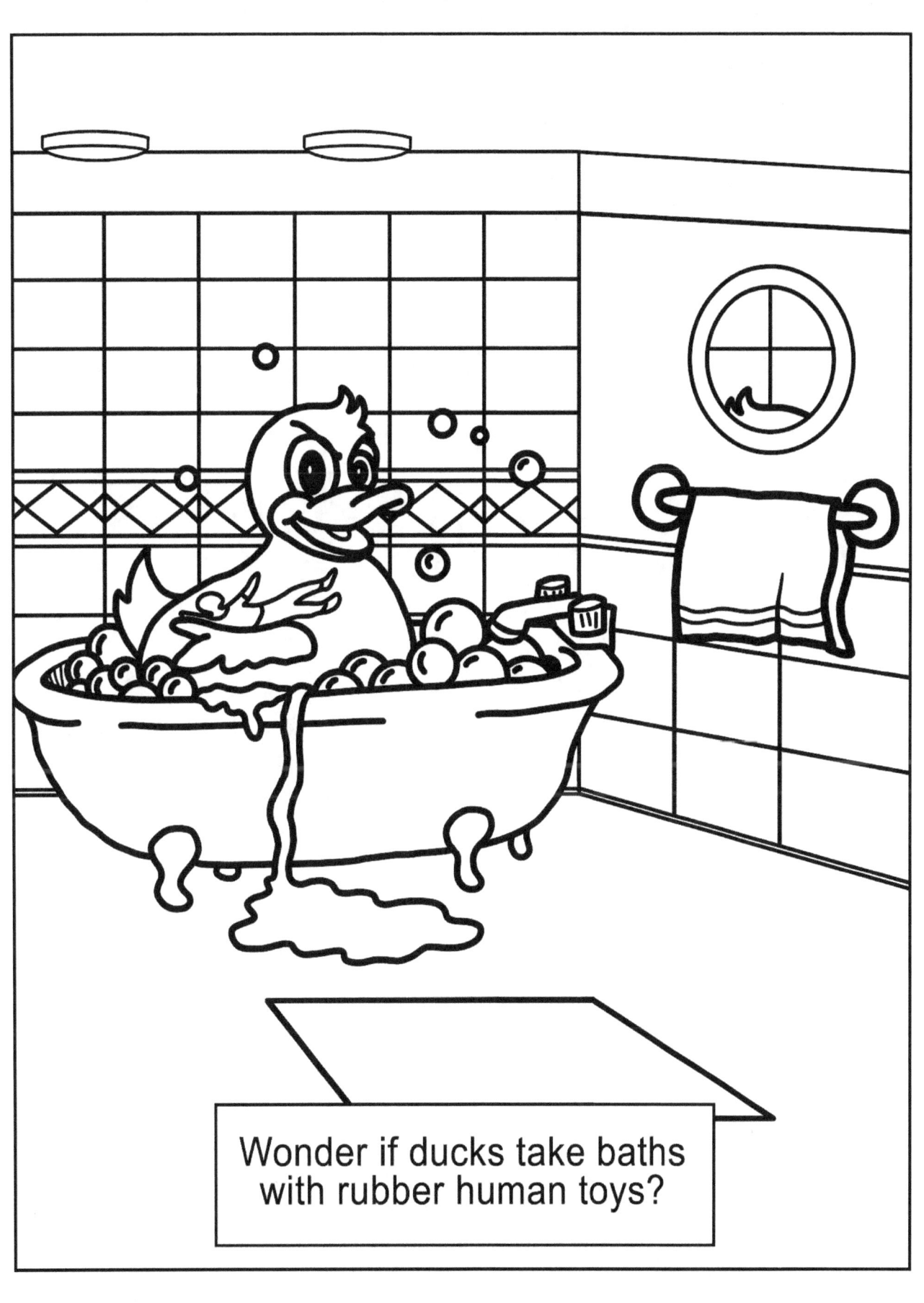

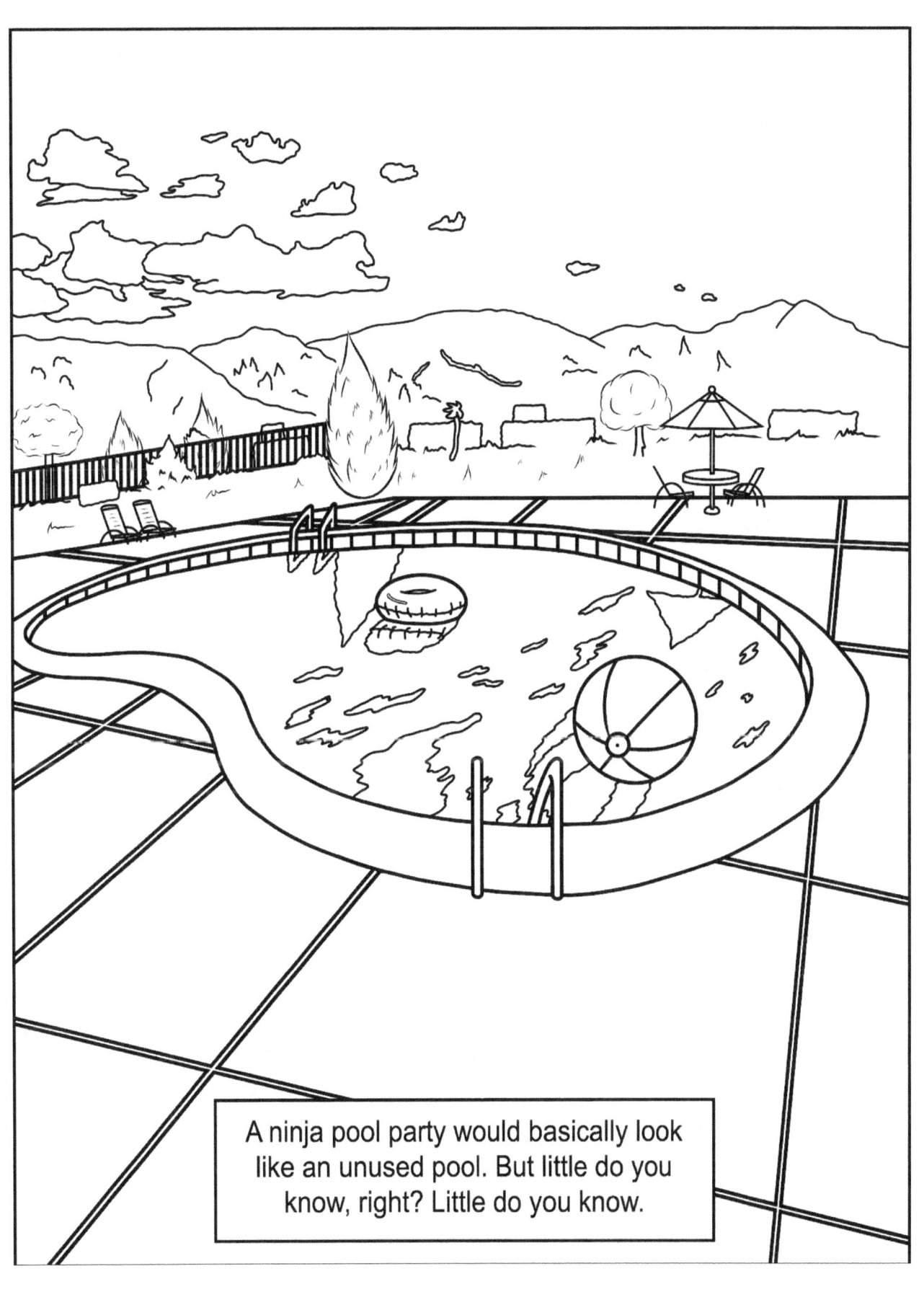

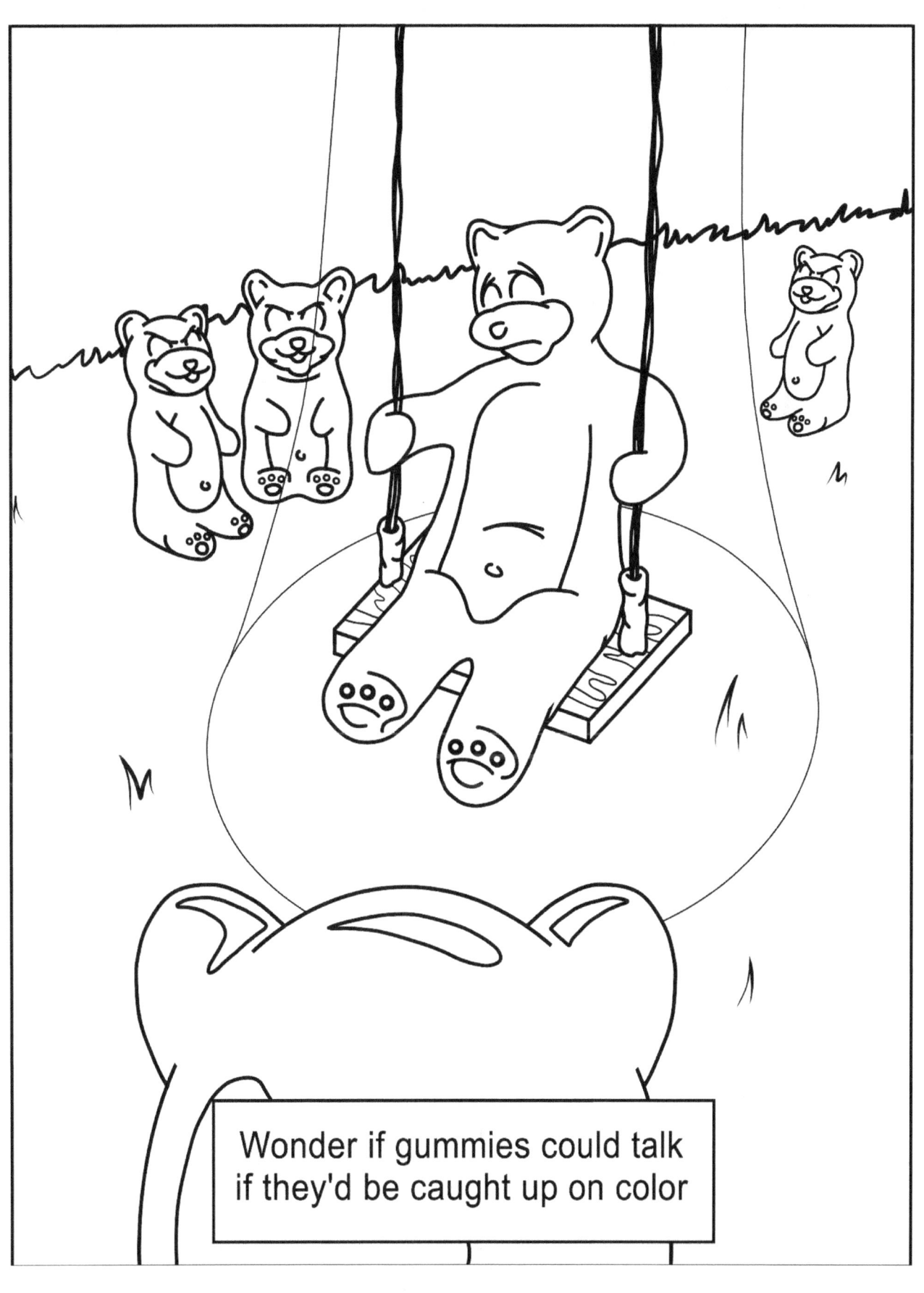

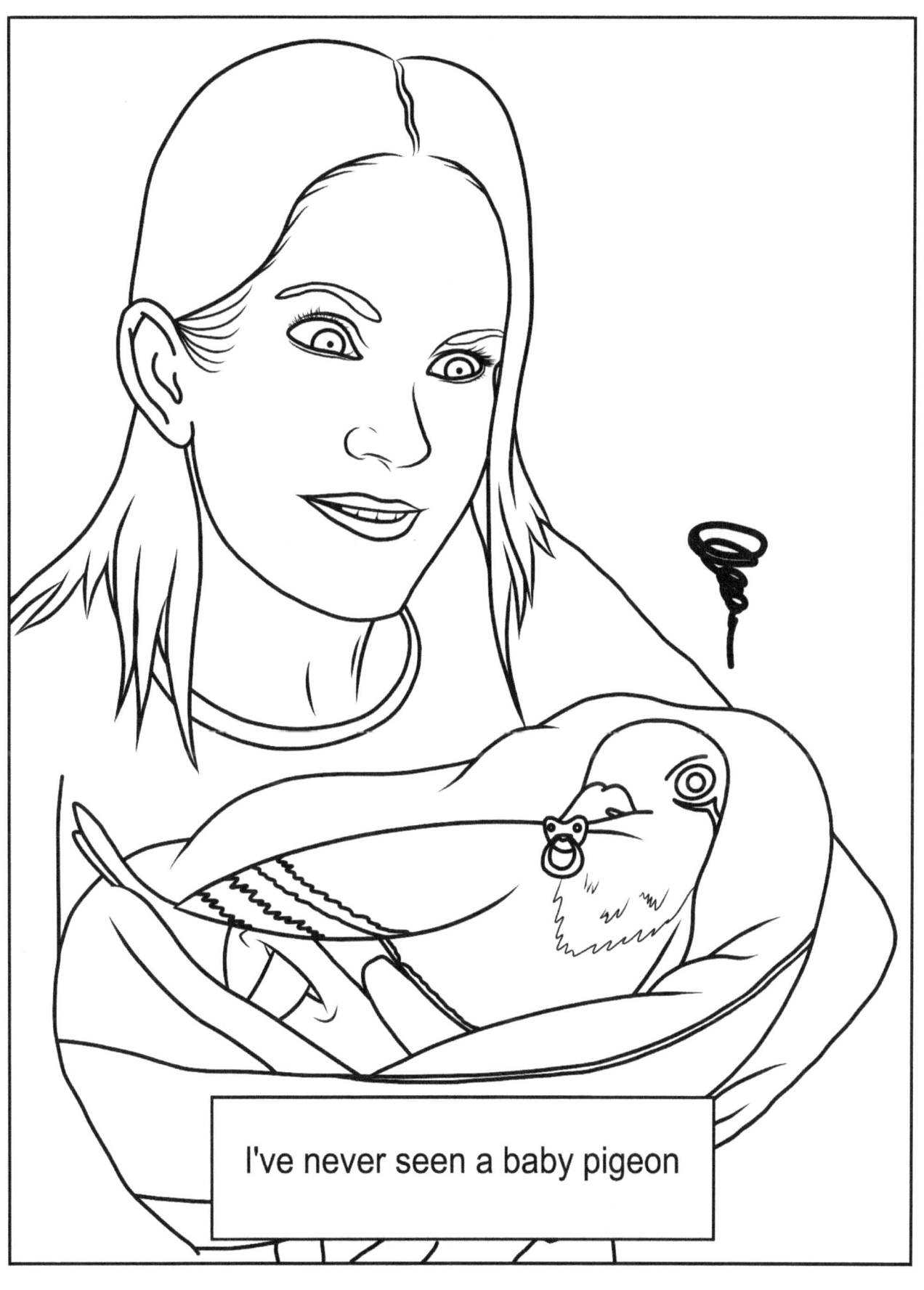

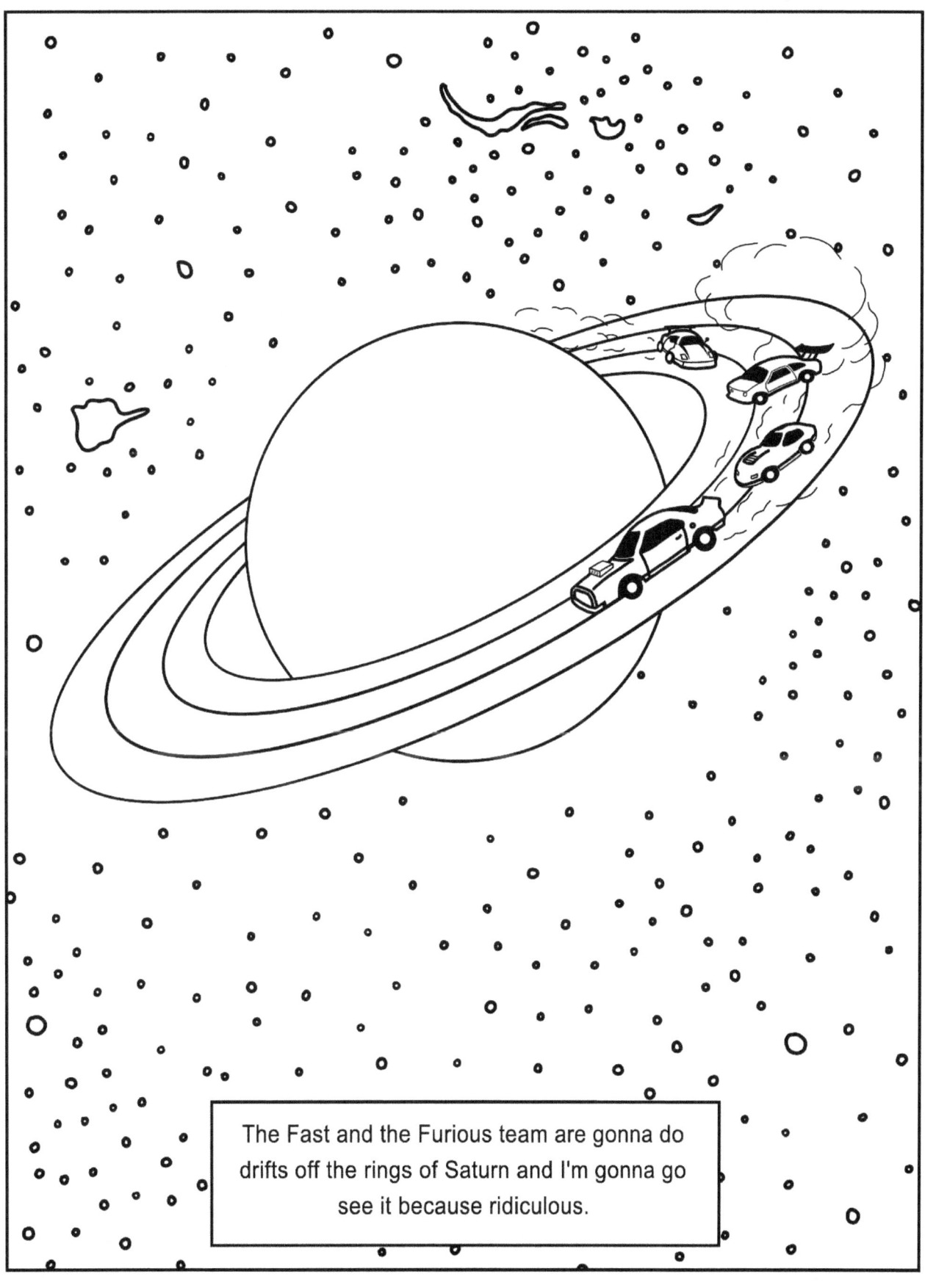

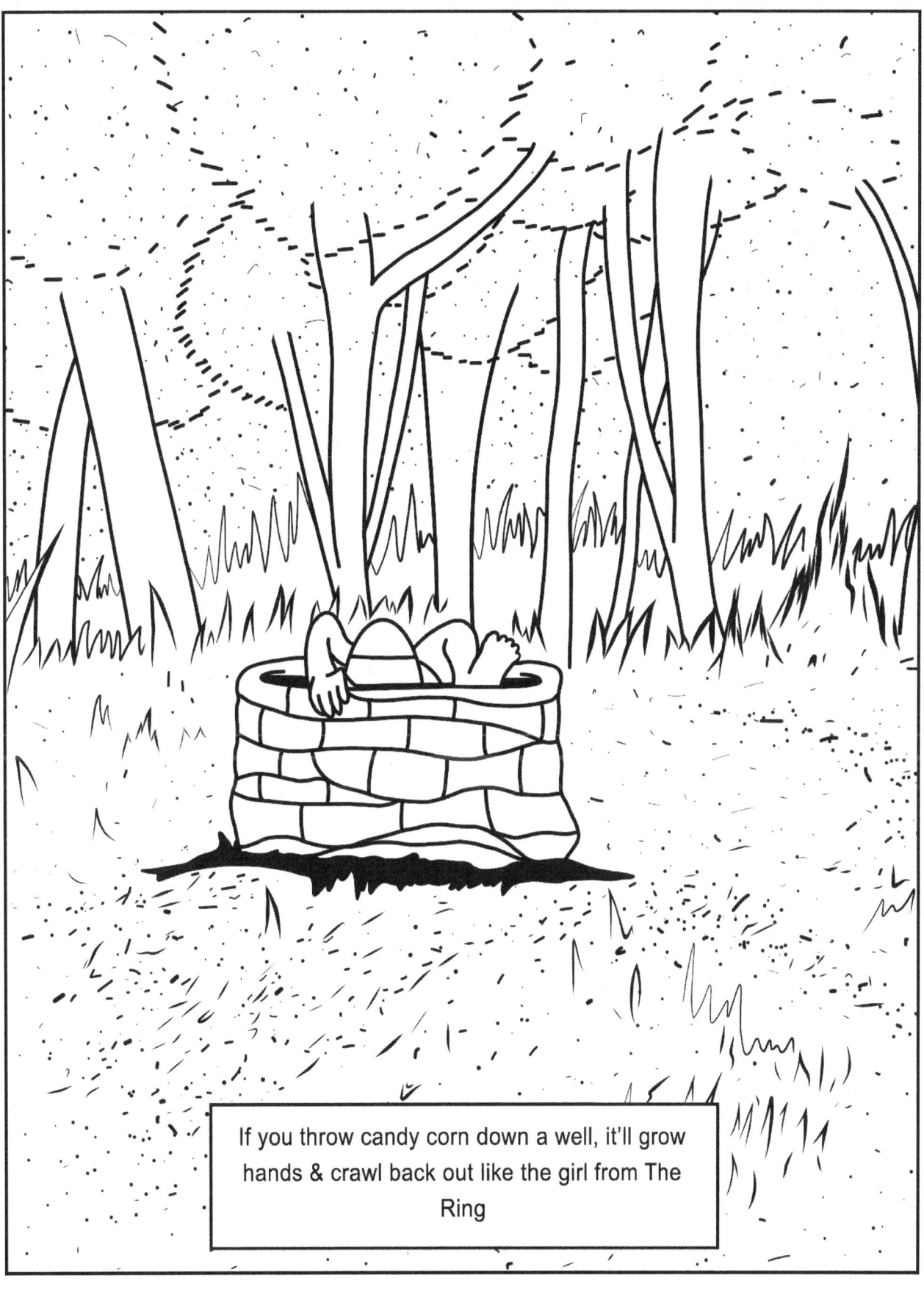

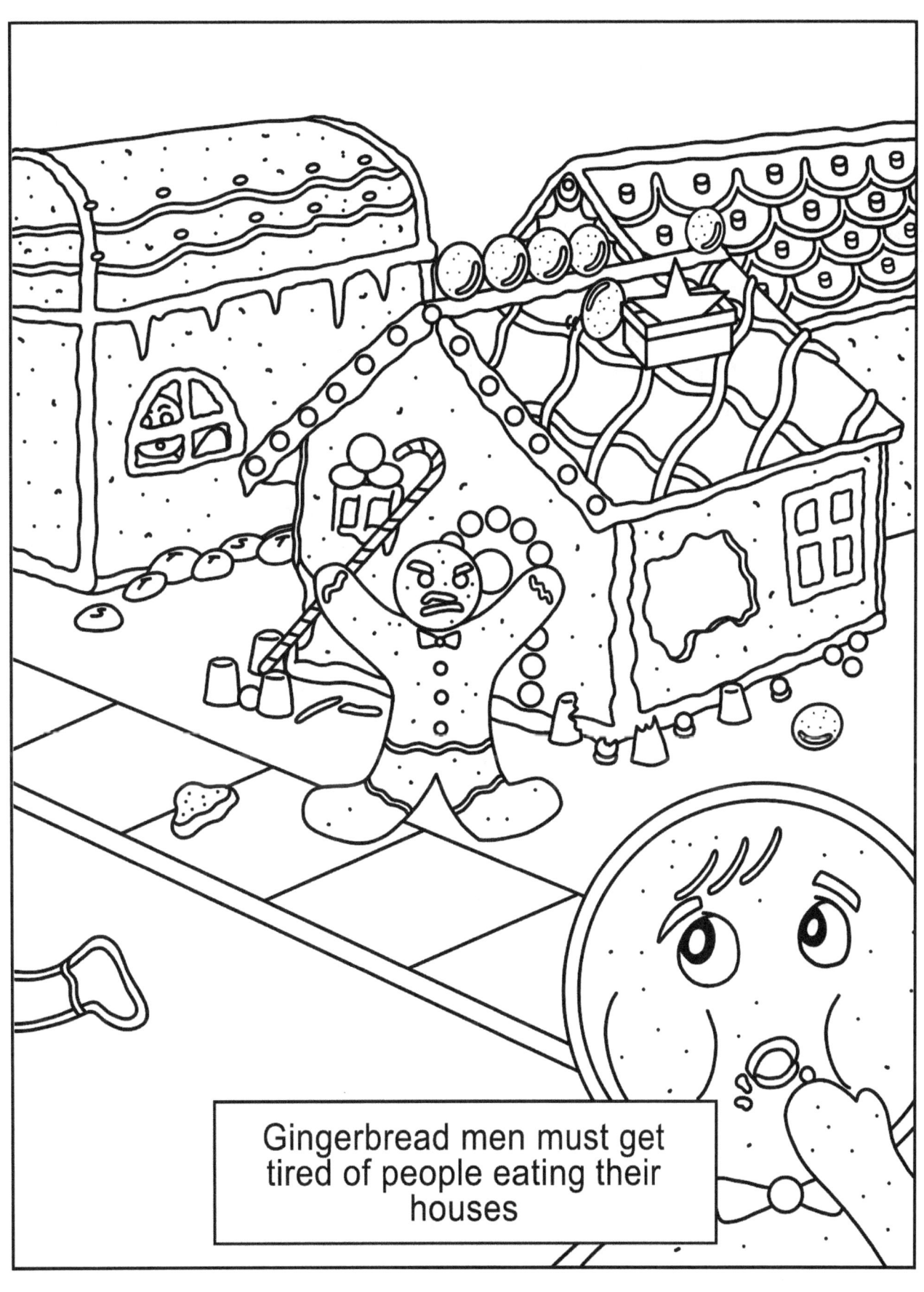

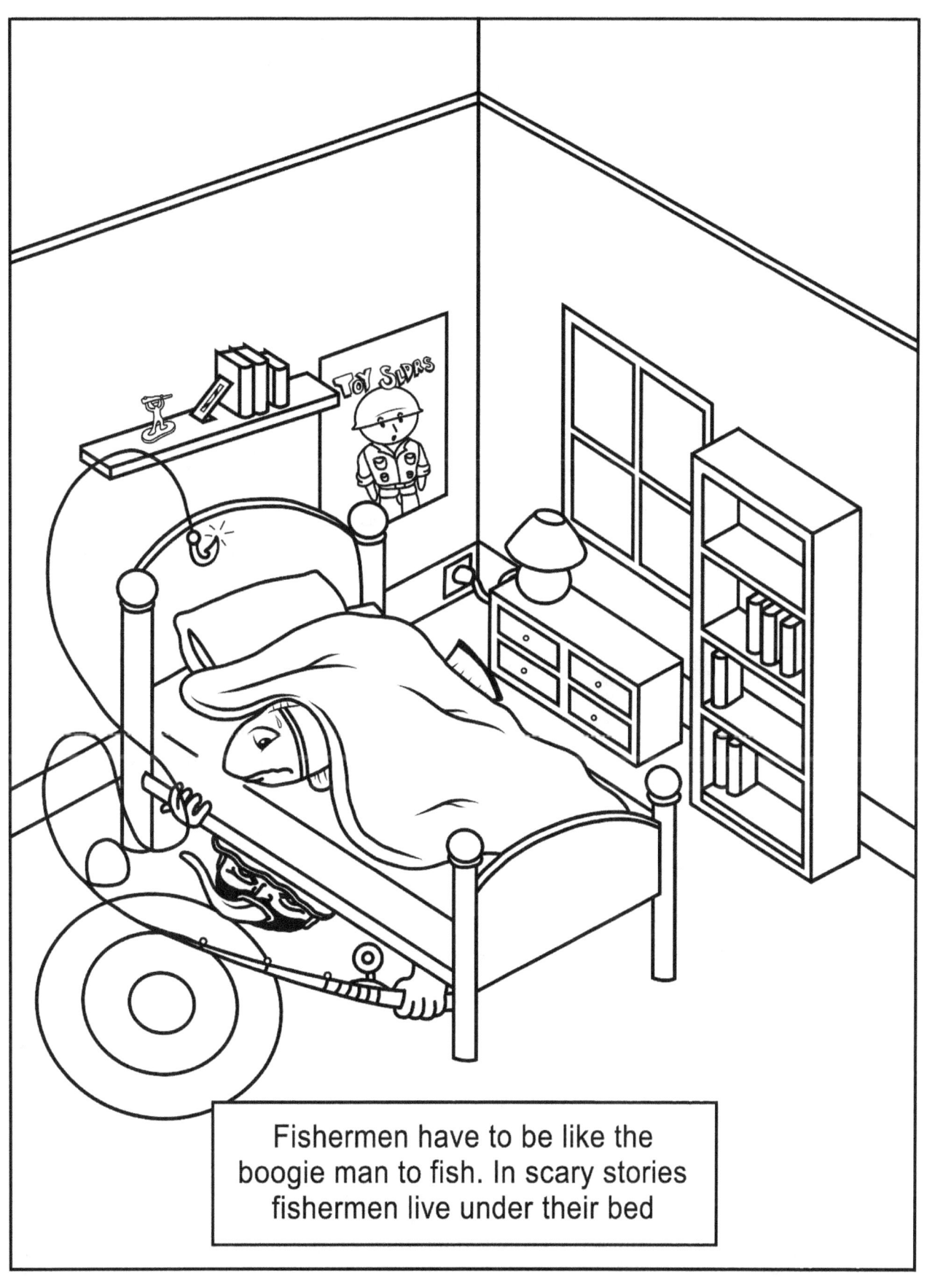

Fishermen have to be like the boogie man to fish. In scary stories fishermen live under their bed

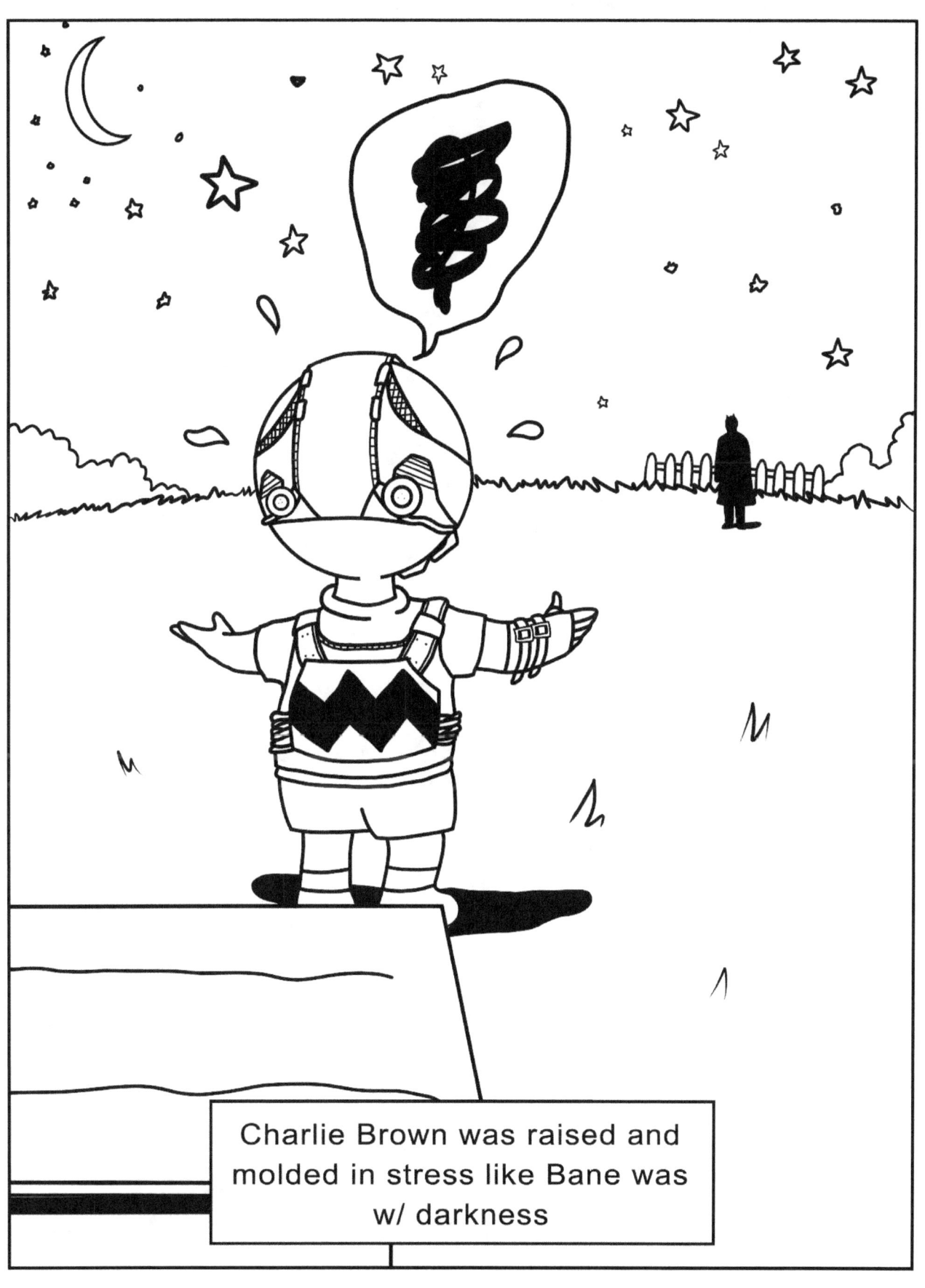

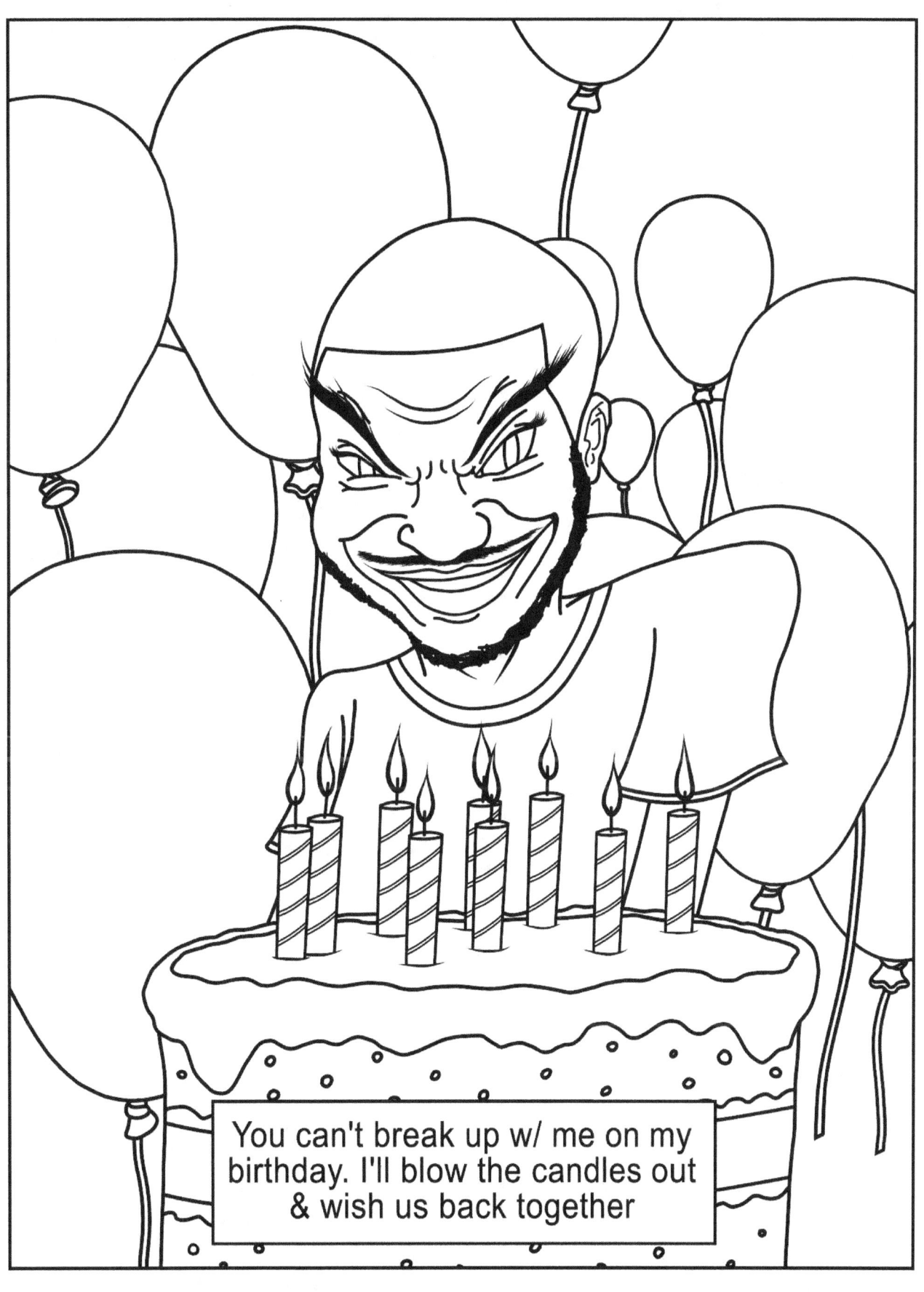

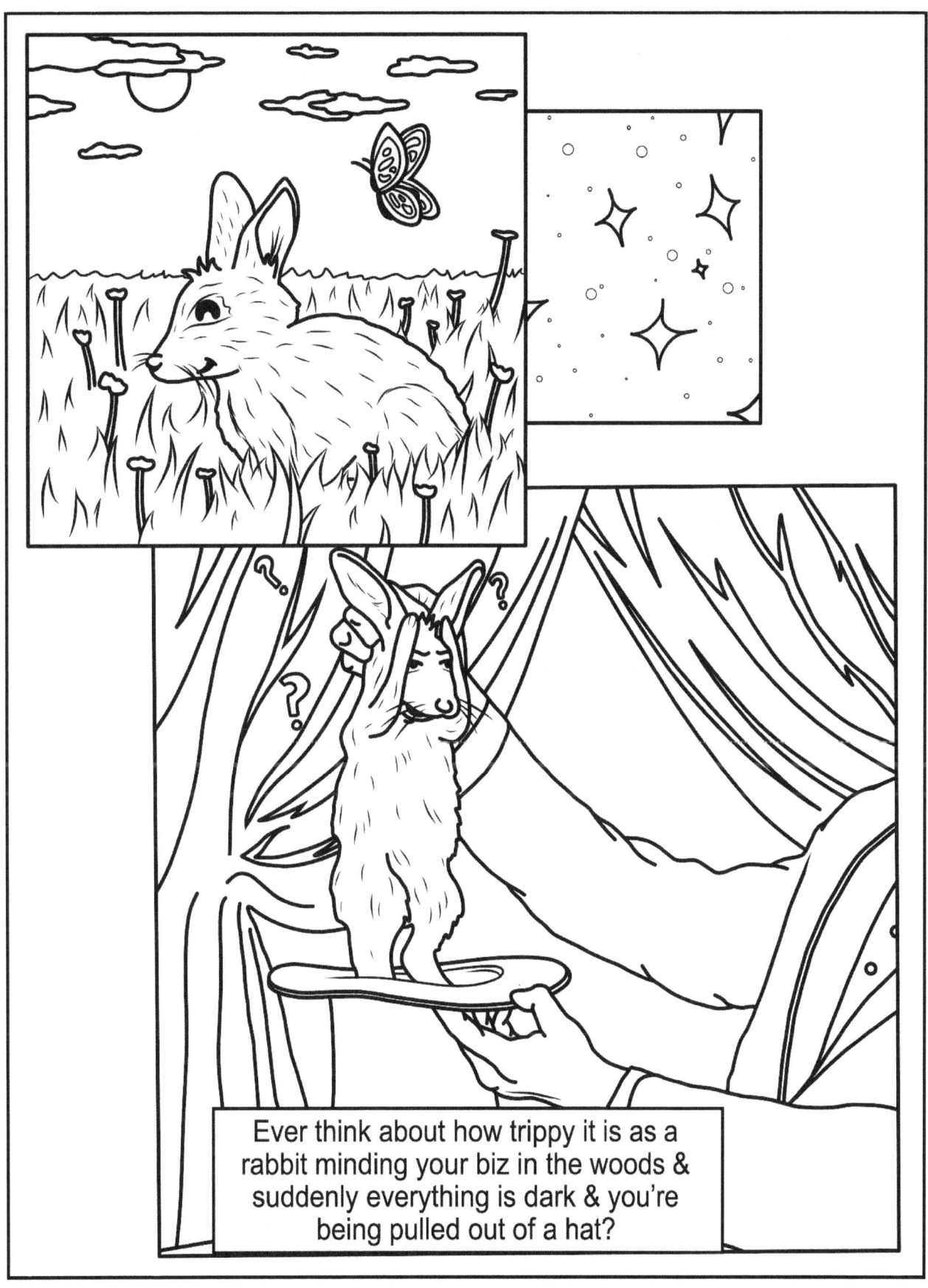

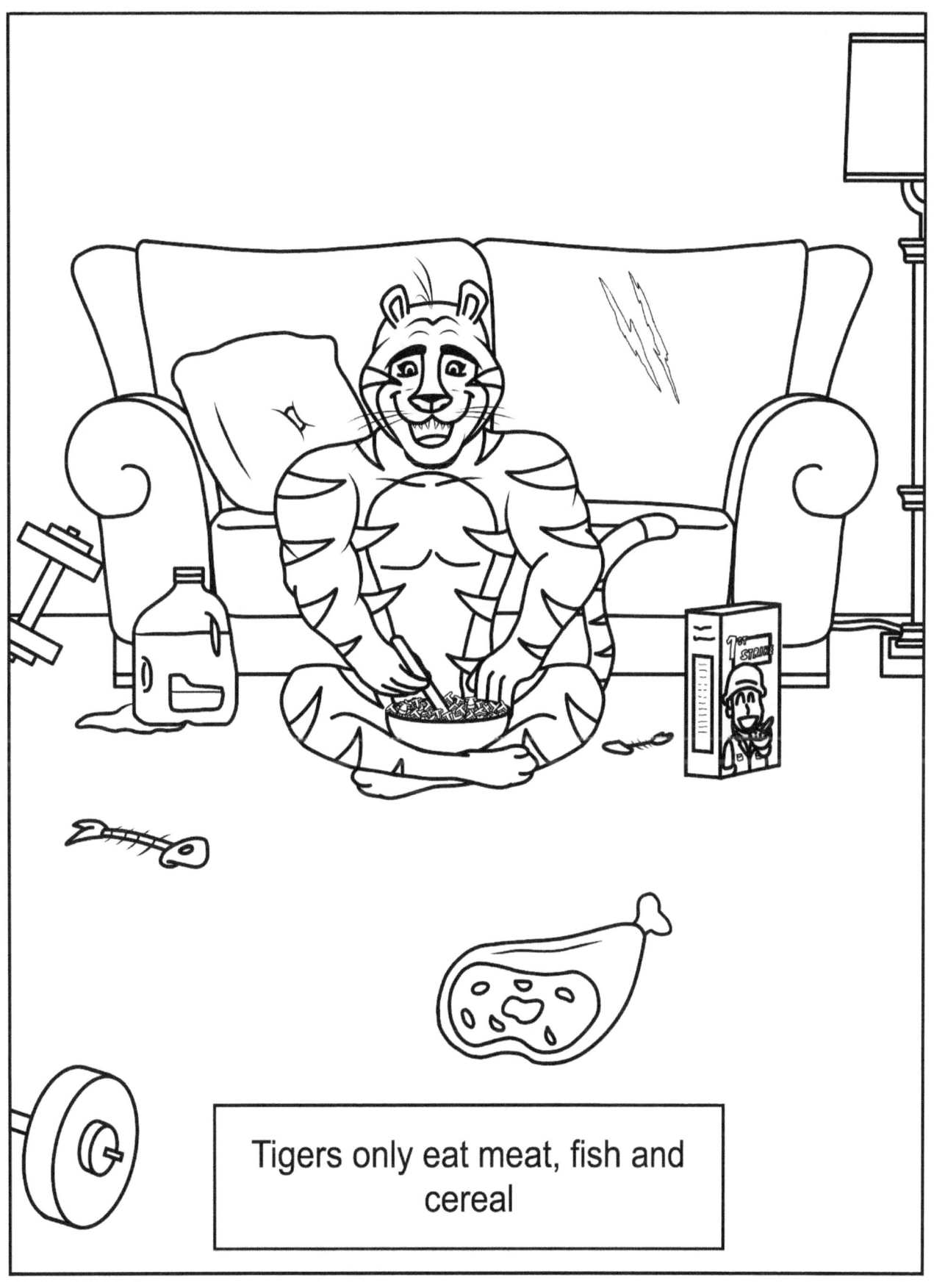

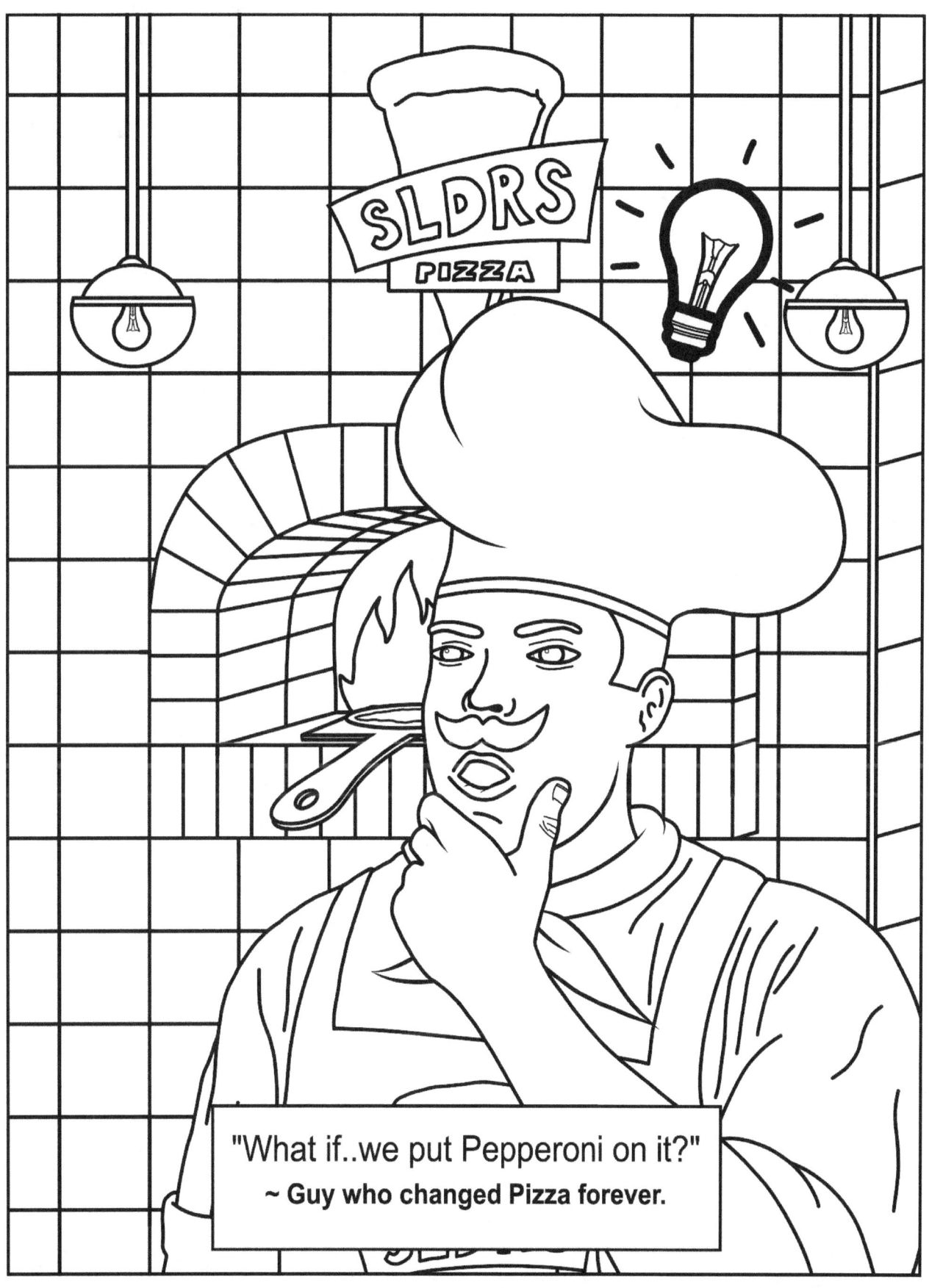

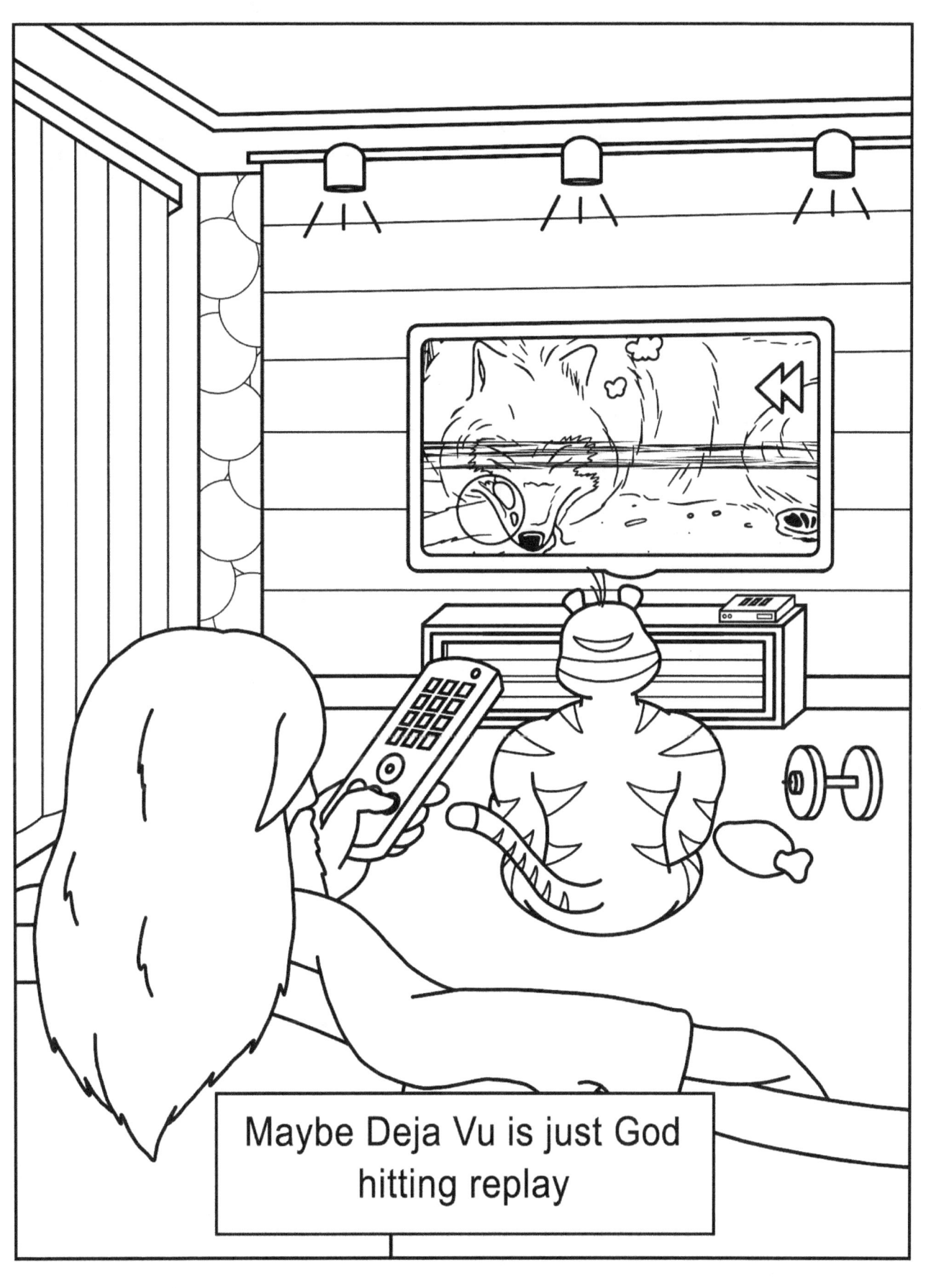

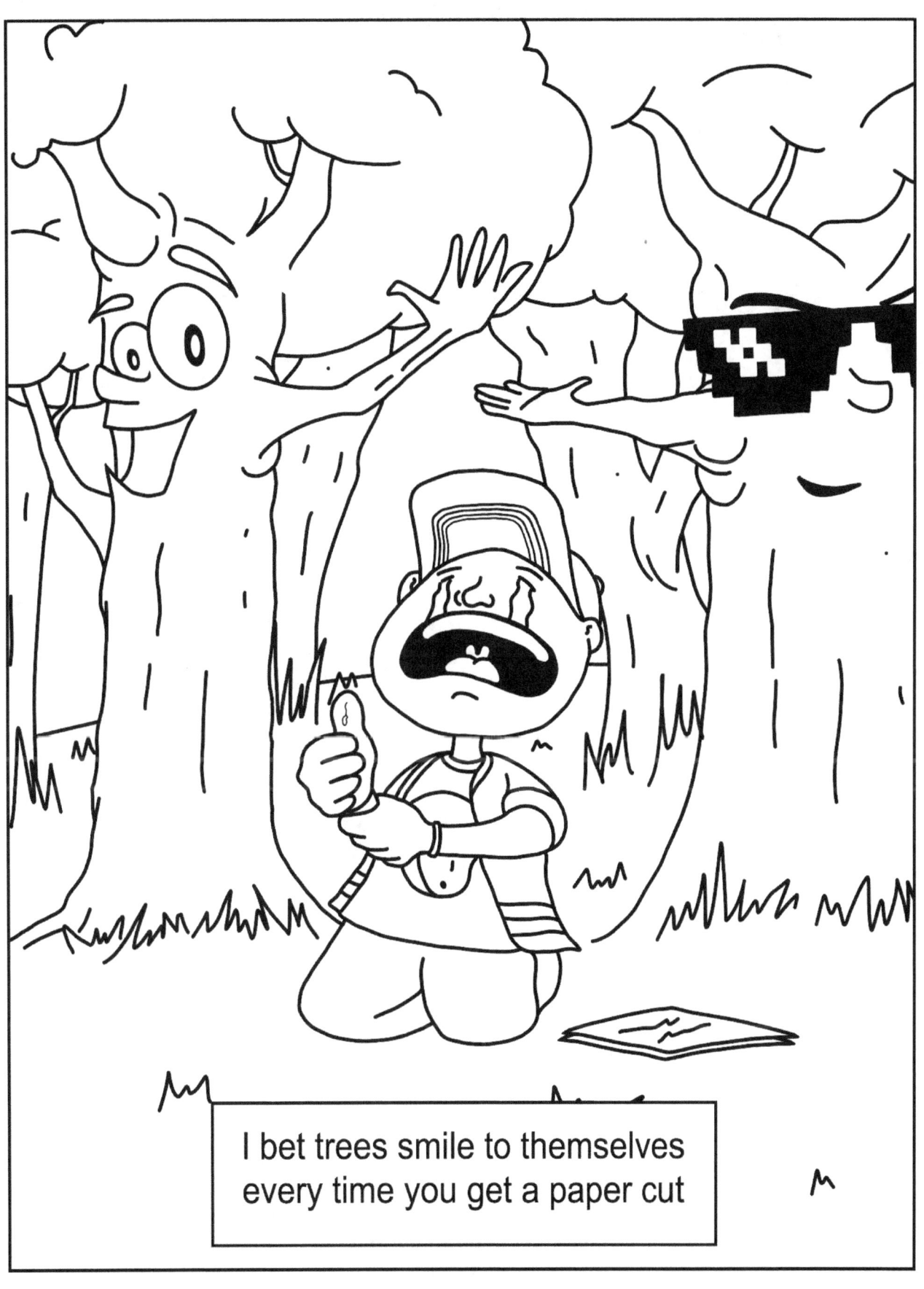

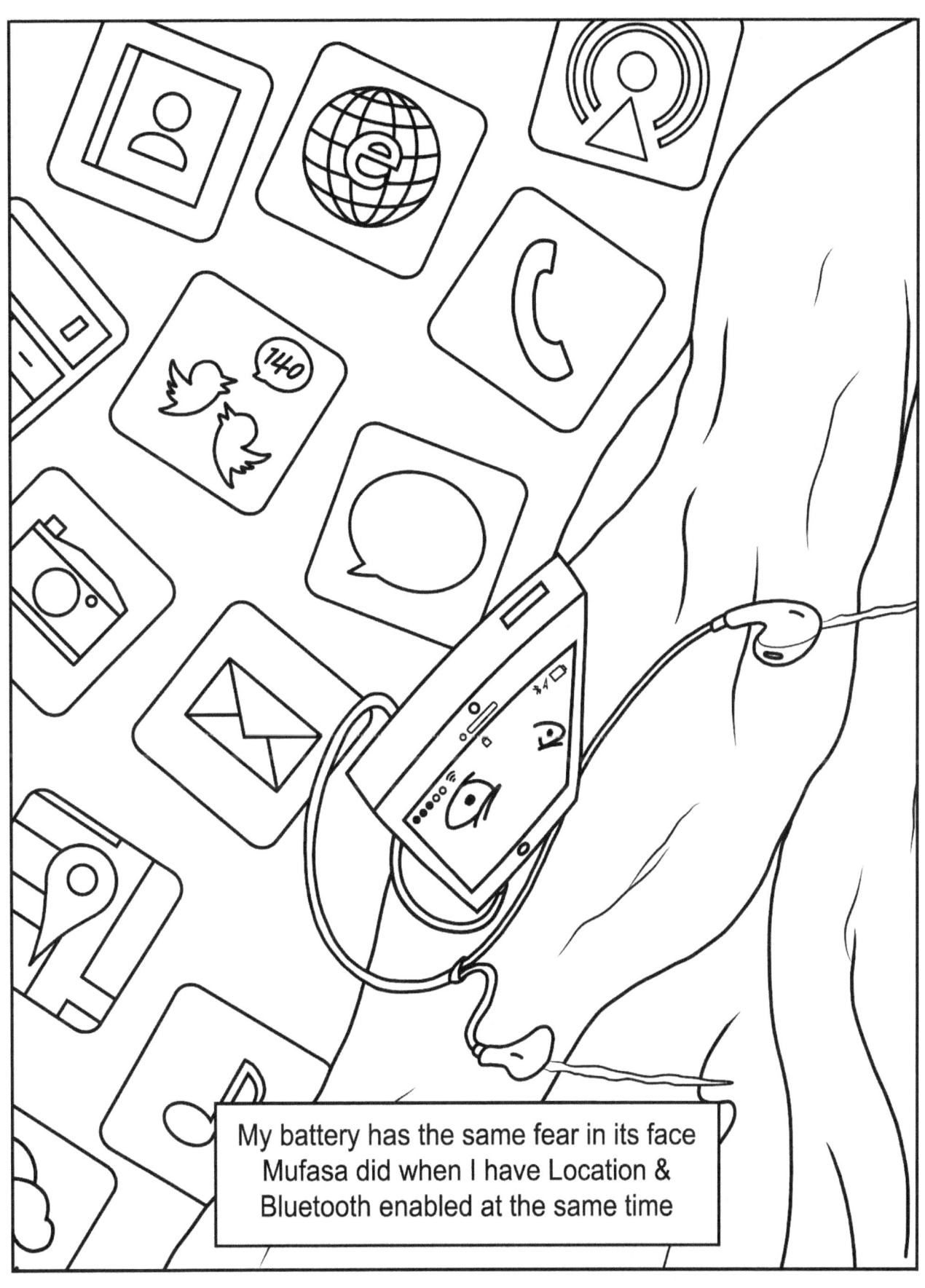

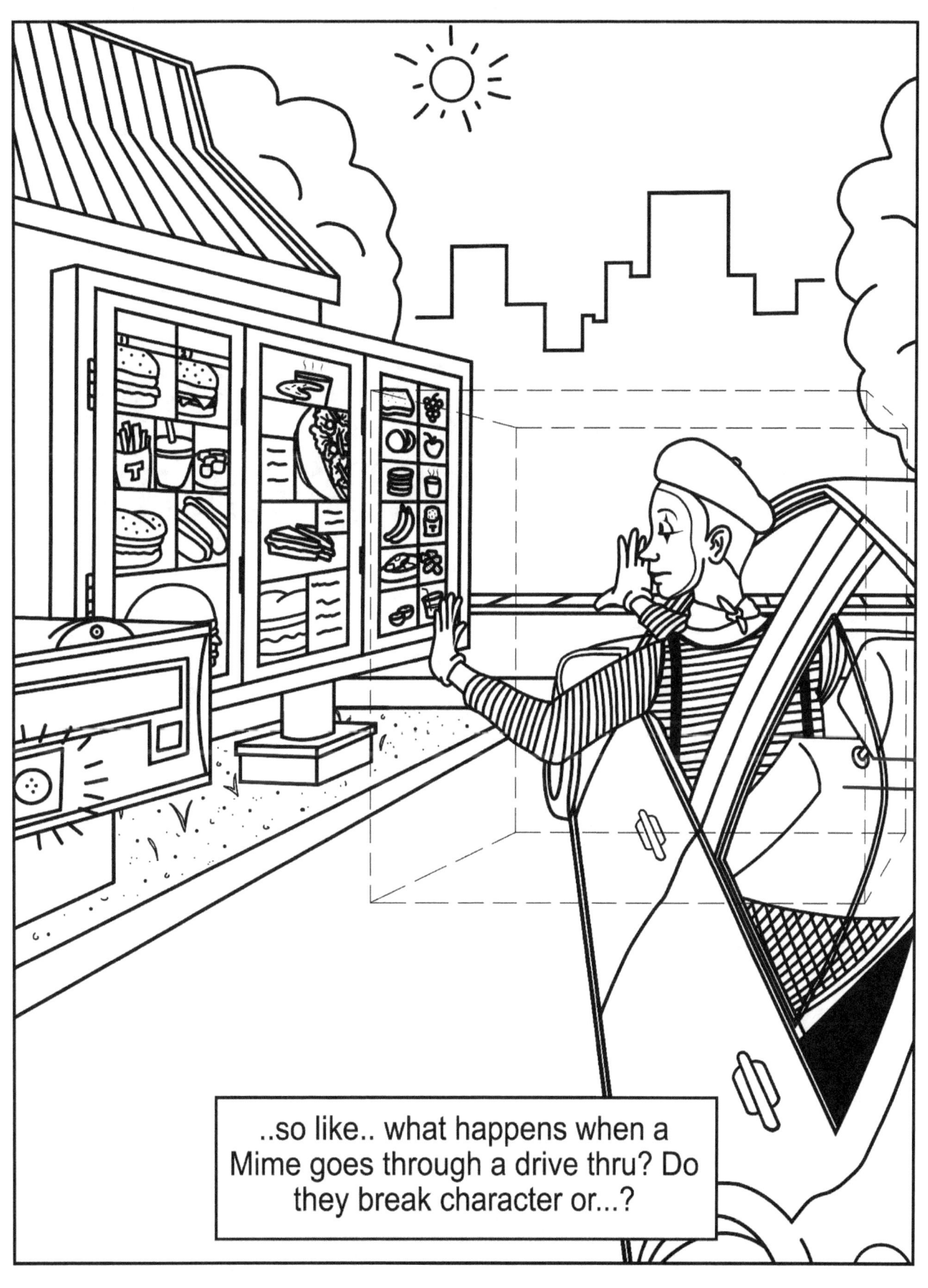

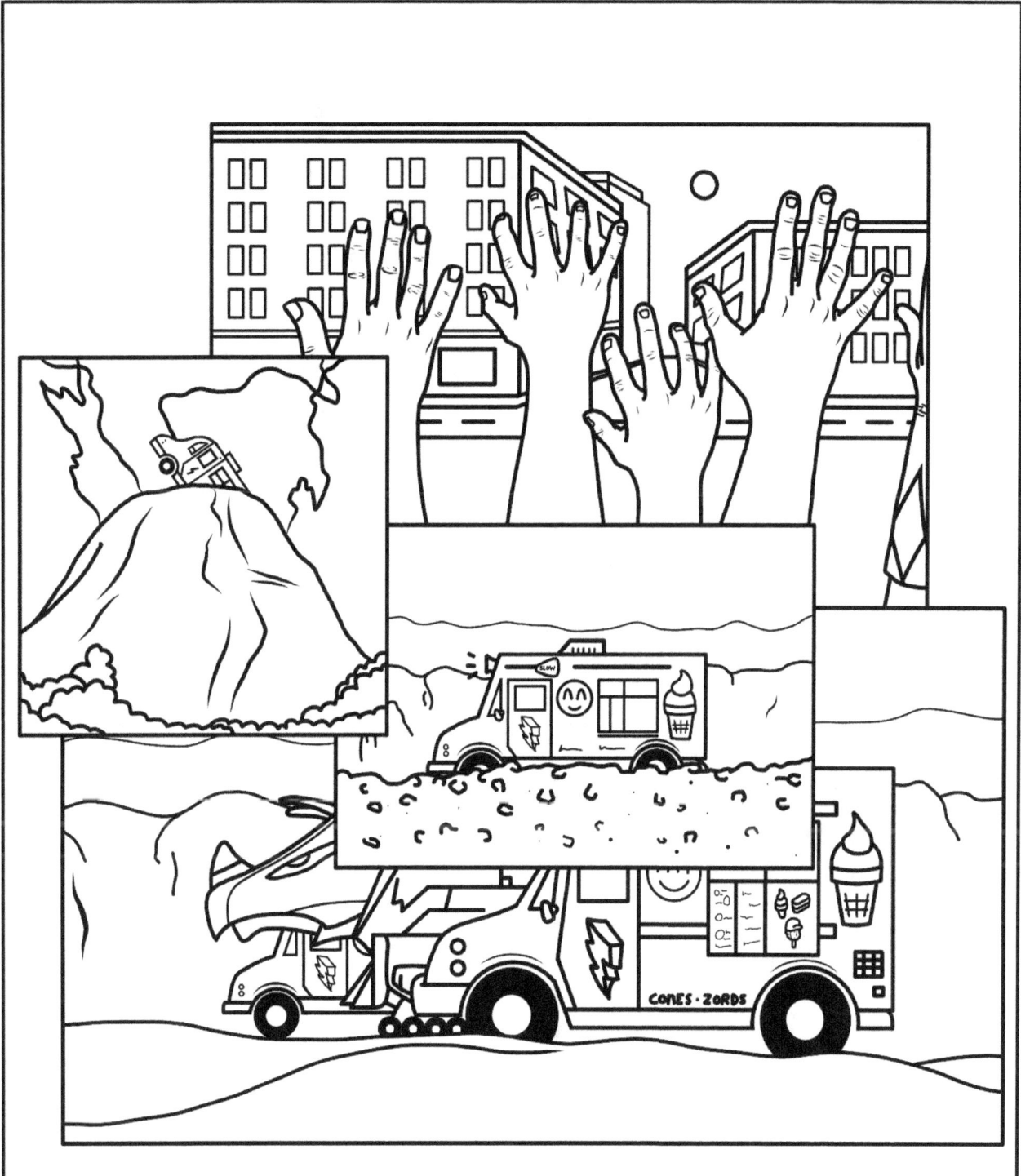

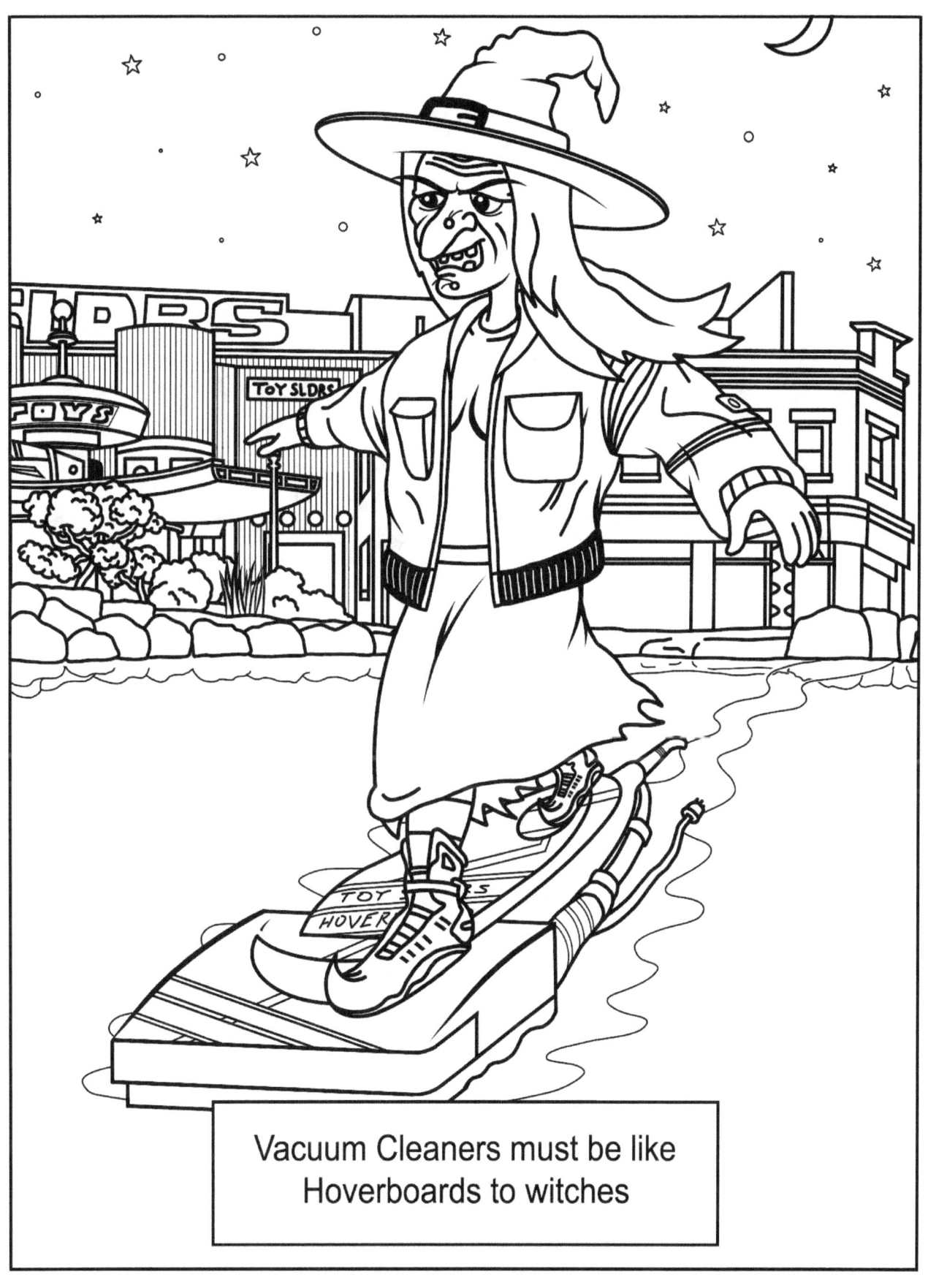

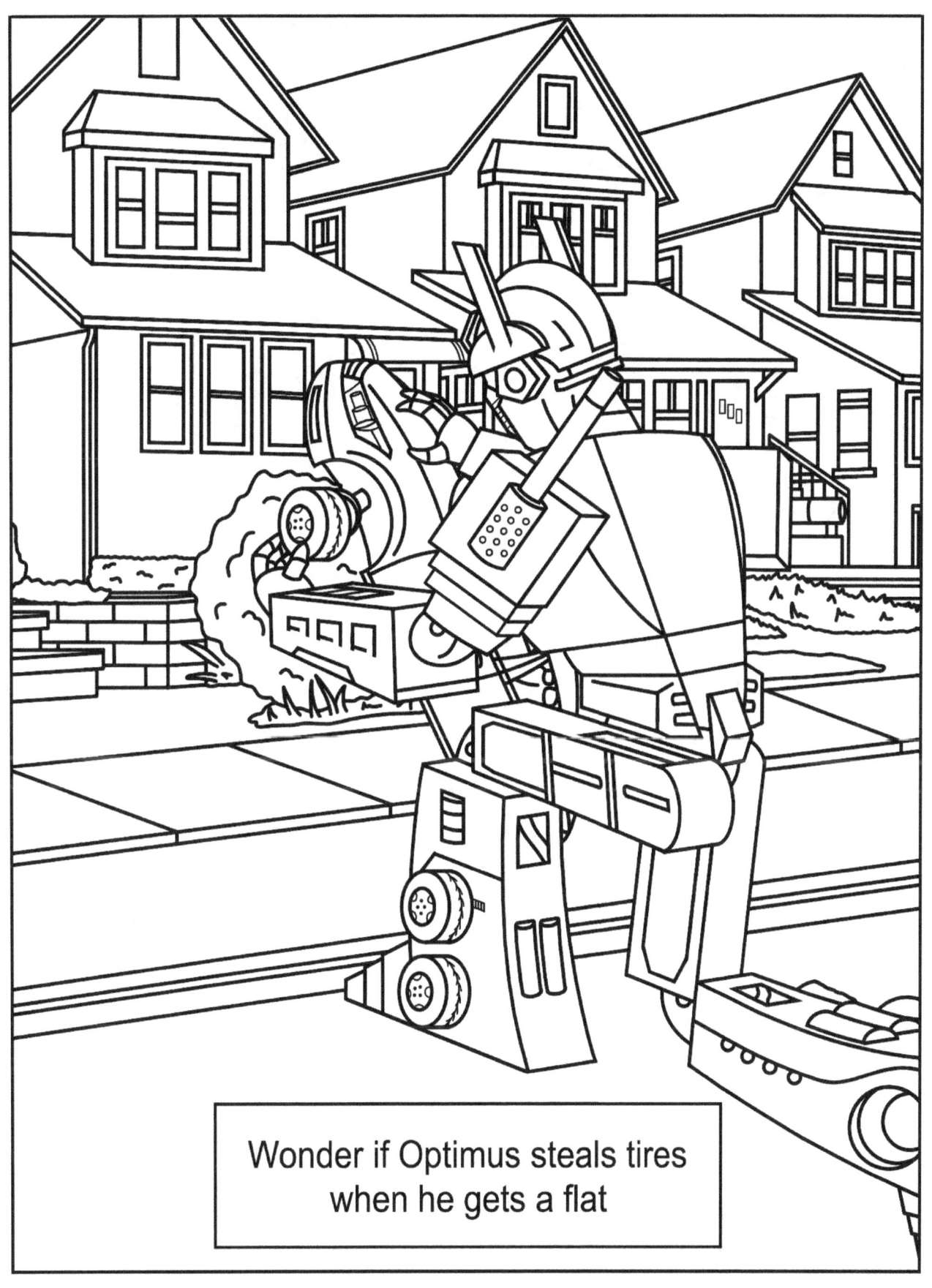

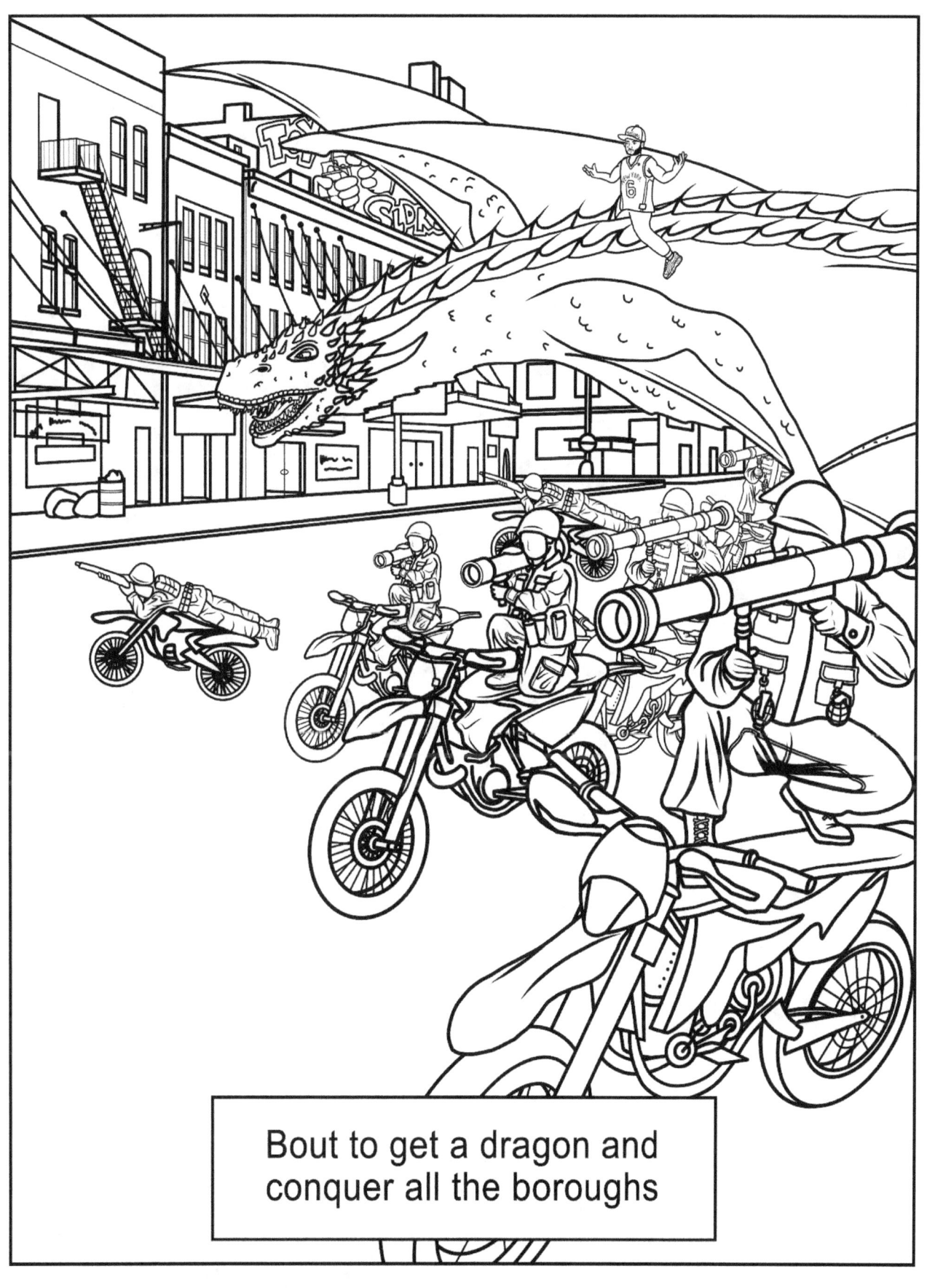

THANK YOU

Hey! Thanks again for your purchase. Did you enjoy the book? Leave a review on Amazon! Comments and ratings help spread the word to others.

Psst! We're on social media! Follow us on
Twitter & Instagram: @ToySldrs

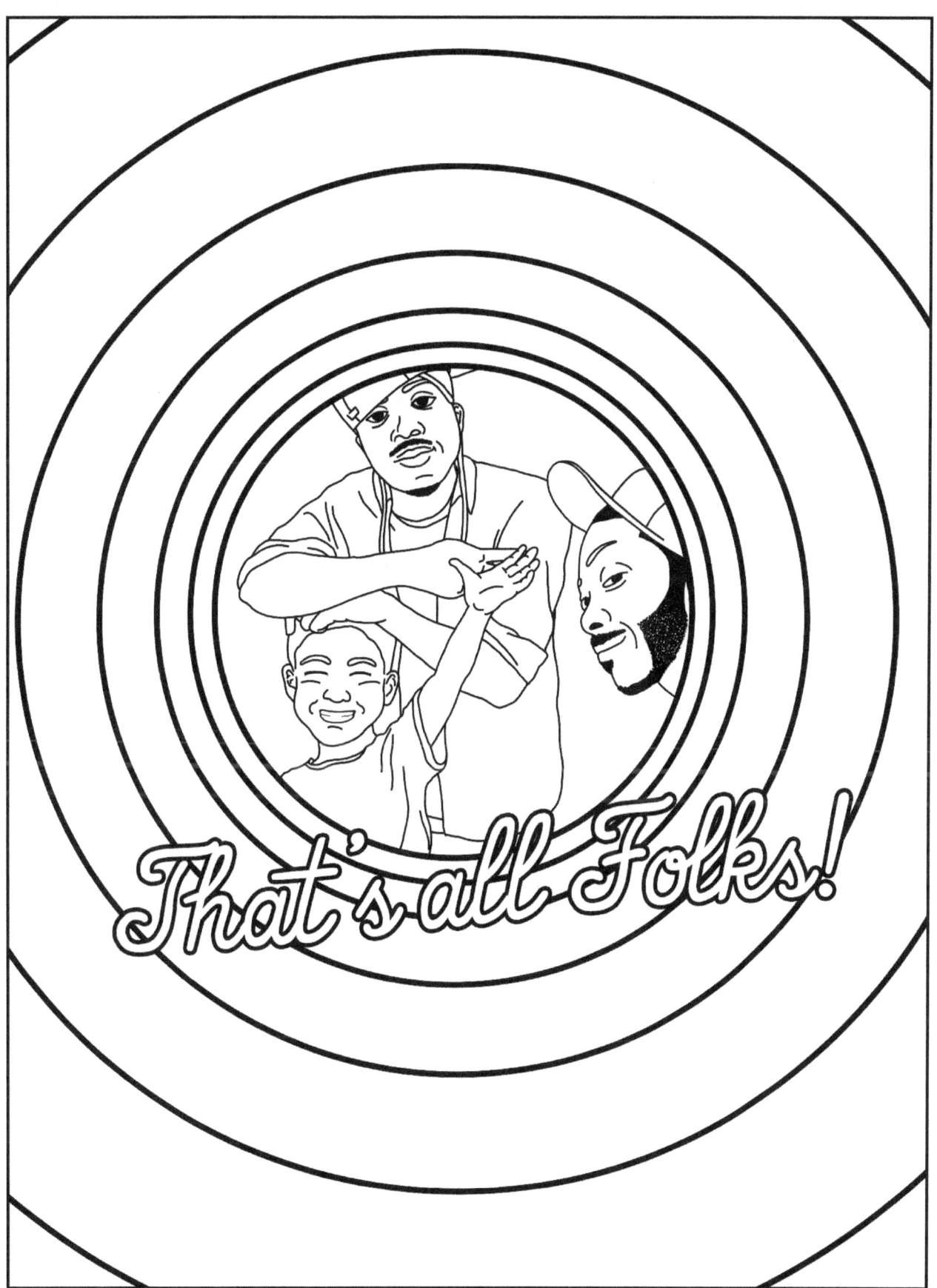

www.ingramcontent.com/pod-product-compliance
Lightning Source LLC
Chambersburg PA
CBHW082357220526
45470CB00008B/2781